OTHER PEOPLE'S *Country*

A woman's journey from suburbia to
remote area nursing

MAUREEN HELEN

ABC
Books

Published by ABC Books for the
AUSTRALIAN BROADCASTING CORPORATION
GPO BOX 9994 Sydney NSW 2001

First published April 2008

National Library of Australia
Cataloguing in Publication entry

Helen, Maureen.
    Other people's country: a woman's journey
    from suburbia to remote area nursing.

    ISBN 978 0 7333 2271 6 (pbk.).

    1. Community health nursing – Western Australia.
    2. Rural health services – Western Australia.
    3. Aboriginal Australians – Western Australia.
    4. Aboriginal Australians – Medical care.
    I. Title. II. Australian Broadcasting Corporation.

610.73430941

Cover design by Christabella Designs
Typeset in 11 on 15pt Bembo by Kirby Jones
Printed by Quality Printing, Hong Kong, China

5 4 3 2 1

Prologue

If it hadn't been for Bangkok, I would never have found myself living and working in an Aboriginal community in a remote part of Western Australia. Before my trip to Thailand, I had thought I was too old and knew, deep down, I was a coward. Fond of being in control, I'd never deliberately set out to take risks I couldn't manage, although I'd moved house and changed jobs often enough to alarm my mother, a bride during the Great Depression years when work was scarce and those who had it hung on to it.

'You need to settle down or no one will give you a job in the future,' she told me on more than one occasion.

In my fifties, I'd begun to think, vaguely, about retirement from the full-time paid workforce. When my last child left home, I was finally free of responsibility for other people, and no longer had a valid excuse to refuse the generous invitations of my sister and brother-in-law to visit them in Thailand, where they'd lived for six years. In our family, Elizabeth had always been regarded as the adventurous one. She thrived on travel to exotic places and enjoyed living in different countries, while I was content in my insular suburban comfort. Besides, raising six children on my own had absorbed much of my energy and most of my money.

'I'm happy being a grandmother; I don't need to travel,' I told Elizabeth several times.

But she was keen to share her enthusiasm with me, and didn't readily take no for an answer. In the end, I plucked up the courage to venture overseas for the first time, but only because my sister promised to take great care of me.

Elizabeth knew her way around. She took me to temples and palaces and markets where we mingled with Thais and tourists. We ventured out on the Chao Phraya River, boarding public ferries laden with locals until the decks were only a few centimetres above oily black water abandoned decades previously by fish and other living creatures.

In longboats we chugged noisily through the networks of canals criss-crossing that Asian Venice, and Elizabeth pointed out opulent royal barges, laying hens confined in parrot cages on poles above the water, naked children swimming beneath slime-covered pylons, coffin-makers at work at the water's edge and plumes of dense black smoke that carried the odour of burning flesh from funeral pyres.

We travelled overnight on the train to Chiang Mai with our purses and passports tucked under our narrow mattresses. We rode elephants that rocked and rolled from side to side as they swung their trunks to feel the slippery terrain in front of them, and then picked their way surprisingly daintily down steep embankments in the rainforests.

'At our age, we should be sitting in rocking chairs,' Elizabeth said, her knuckles white as she gripped the saddle in front of her, but I knew she didn't mean it.

In the life-threatening pollution of Bangkok traffic, we rode in death-defying motorised vehicles with soft tops and no sides or doors. They were identified by the 'tuk-tuk' noise they made. The drivers were young men; they thought themselves invincible and didn't give a damn that their passengers knew they were not. We were soaked to the skin with perspiration and, in the narrow side streets, or *sois*, drenched with water flung at us and other bystanders from the buckets of exuberant youngsters celebrating Songkran, the annual Thai water festival.

In a city constantly in the process of remaking itself, footpaths were potholed and drains exposed. Everywhere, buildings were being demolished and others hurriedly erected, while workers and their families lived hazardous lives on floors already completed.

A Redemptorist priest, originally from North America, took us on a tour of his extensive parish in the Klong Toey slums. Docks that curved around the Chao Phraya River contained the district on one side; twelve-lane highways with their constant cacophony of Bangkok traffic defined the other boundaries. Shanties built on rotting boardwalks over hectares of swampy ground collapsed against each other. Household waste and untreated sewage ran in filthy uncovered drains between and under the shacks and makeshift walkways.

Crowded there together, thousands of people lived, and many died, day after day. Grandmothers, themselves wasted and lethargic, cared for tiny waifs whose parents had abandoned them or died from HIV/AIDS. Even the rats slinking along in the mud in full view were skinny, unlike the fat, furry rats of the more affluent areas of the city.

Through the openings into tiny windowless rooms, we saw elderly women and little girls huddled together, picking over old rags or crocheting white cotton into lace.

'These are the lucky ones,' the priest told us. 'They earn a few cents a day.'

Deep in the slum, we came across a crowd of men milling around, shouting excitedly. Some held squawking roosters by their feet.

'We need to get out,' our priestly guide said urgently. He jostled us roughly back the way we'd come. 'Cockfighting! They're vicious,' he explained when he thought we were safe. 'The birds *and* the men.'

In an open-air abattoir surrounded by shanties, pigs were slaughtered for the Bangkok markets. Ear-splitting squeals competed with the snarl of traffic. Fresh blood and pig shit ran into the drains. A sharp ferric odour dominated the stench of human and animal excreta that hung over everything. We watched a diminutive Catholic nun in a grey habit and rubber thongs shuffling through bloodied puddles to a shack where, we were told, she lived alone on the other side of the slaughter yard.

For years I'd made a fuss about social justice. I'd read liberation theology, donated to aid programs in Third World countries, and protested vociferously in the name of different causes. But while these activities stemmed from a genuinely held personal philosophy and ethical position, the underbelly of Bangkok confronted me in a visceral, visual, demanding way I'd never before experienced. Gradually the idea of working in such a place took hold, though only as a nebulous, romantic vision. Perhaps, I thought, I could make a difference, if only to the lives of a handful of people.

But back home in Perth, I knew I didn't have the confidence to leave my family, which included two small granddaughters, Claire and Jane. The idea of performing heroic deeds among poverty-stricken strangers in far-off countries faded, and I settled back into my comfortable old patterns that included a rewarding career as a family counsellor, a large and growing family, and a satisfying social life. I managed to compartmentalise my recent experience and unspecified desire, and pretend nothing special had happened.

Then one day at work, I met a young woman from the Coonanna Aboriginal community. Experiencing a complicated pregnancy, she'd been sent from a regional hospital to deliver her baby in Perth. The things she told me about her people and her country on the Nullarbor Plain fascinated me.

Wanting to know more, I read in a book in the library that early in the twentieth century a mission had been established at Cundalee, north of Coonanna. When the missionaries withdrew, the whole community moved to the new site at Coonanna, a few kilometres north of the railway line that crosses Australia from the Indian Ocean to the Pacific. After a few years of good management, the settlement boasted pastoral and horticultural enterprises, market gardens and even a grassed football oval, in spite of a severe water shortage. Around 400 people lived there permanently.

Weeks after my encounter with the young woman, the word 'Coonanna' stood out — the way new words tend to when you've recently learned them — in a newspaper advertisement for a remote area community nurse, and my longings for adventure reignited. Three registered nurses, with the help of several Aboriginal health workers, staffed the nursing post at Coonanna.

I was a registered nurse and midwife, and although most of my experience had been in hospital wards and management, I'd once worked as a community nurse in a high school in the Perth metropolitan area. And there'd be a team of colleagues I could learn from. I'd be able to travel home for weekends by train via Kalgoorlie. I could have an adventure while I did something that would matter. I applied for the position.

My application was rejected. I wasn't sure whether I was relieved or devastated, and alternated between the two states for a week or so. Then I shelved my fantasy and was again absorbed back into my ordinary life.

Months later, when I'd almost forgotten my dream, I was offered a position at a place called Jigalong in Palyku country.

'Yes,' I said immediately. 'Yes, please.'

Common sense should have demanded that I give the proposal more thought, or at least ask why they'd offered me a job for which I hadn't applied. But it probably wouldn't have made much difference to my decision, even had I known then that government departments described Jigalong as a difficult-to-staff location, or that teachers were offered special allowances and incentives to work at Jigalong Primary School. It was a two-nurse post, although the population there was around 400, the same as that at Coonanna.

I couldn't even locate Jigalong on the first map I consulted. When I eventually pinpointed it on one with more detail, I was appalled that I'd already agreed to go there. The place was in the middle of Western Australia, on the edge of a desert and far from any town. Trips home would be limited. I'd never lived away from family and friends before, so the separation would be a major challenge. But I convinced myself that Jigalong sounded magical, even better than Coonanna. This was an amazing opportunity.

One of my daughters did not want me to go and my sons told me bluntly that I was mad, but I detected a note of pride in their voices. After all, not many mothers my age did anything half as reckless. They told me I'd have an exciting time and wished me well. Some of my friends warned me with considerable insight about the difficulties and dangers I'd face, especially as a woman on my own, living in an Aboriginal settlement.

Ignoring them all, and in spite of growing misgivings, in 1991 I went to work at the Jigalong Aboriginal settlement with a mixture of open curiosity, missionary zeal and a craving for excitement. It was the roller-coaster adventure of my life. I left home thinking I could be a small part of the solution to endemic Aboriginal ill-health, with its disgraceful morbidity and mortality rates. That was a big mistake; my simplistic idealism denied the history, complexity and extent of the problems.

I was unprepared emotionally, physically or professionally for what lay ahead. Memories of the details about what happened while I was at Jigalong come and go, and I'm sure I've forgotten many things. Although the heat, dust and isolation might also frame the accounts of other people who were there, the tales we tell would be different. What I am certain of are the challenges, shocks and threats, as well as the delight and wonder that I experienced. In the months that I worked and lived at Jigalong I learned a great deal and confronted rather more than I'd bargained for. This is the story of my time in the desert.

I

The plane touches down and bumps along yet another red runway, but this time there's a well-lit passenger terminal across the tarmac and the flight attendant announces we have arrived at Port Hedland. It's the fourth time we've landed since leaving Perth. The locals call this the milk-run trip because of the frequent stops and starts that allow the plane to set down and pick up mailbags and passengers at tiny Pilbara mining towns on the way to its destination. Most of the other travellers are mining or construction workers, ready for their next shift by the look of their work shorts and steel-capped boots, and there is a scattering of thin, weather-beaten women and grizzling, overtired children.

Caught in a skirmish of impatient passengers pushing and shoving and foraging in overhead lockers for bags and parcels, I shuffle to the door at the front of the plane, thank the flight attendants poised formally at the exit, and step out onto the gantry.

Outside our protective aluminium container, the September evening is also cocooned. At first sight it seems uterine, although it could herald a bloodbath. The sky swells crimson as the last rays of the fugitive sun reflect off lava particles hurled into the atmosphere from the erupting Mt Pinatubo in the Philippines. Below, rusty earth stretches into treeless distance.

I'd anticipated desert when I got to Jigalong, not at Port Hedland. I thought this first stop on my journey would be ordinary, more like home. Instead, it's a strange space that manages to be claustrophobic and gaping wide at the same time. I look for signs of fear or anxiety on the faces of my fellow passengers, but none of them seems to notice anything out of the ordinary in this eerie dusk that's seeping across the landscape.

On the gangway, I breathe burning air and taste dust. On the tarmac, my sandals fill with dirt and my feet are gritty. Off the bitumen path, there's no grass, no softening. Before I reach the terminal, I'm gasping for oxygen and panicked by the red heat that compresses my lungs. The long low utilitarian building, all glass and noise, is white-lit and air-conditioned. Inside, I feel safe and inhale deeply, relieved that I can.

A young, freckle-faced woman in shorts and a striped T-shirt strides towards me.

'You must be the new Jigalong nurse,' she says, smiling a welcome. 'I've come to take you to the flat.'

'Flat?' I repeat. I don't understand and feel stupid.

'It belongs to the department. It's where you'll stay for the few days before you go to Jigalong. Didn't they tell you?'

'No,' I say. 'I thought I'd be in a motel. And I expected to make my own way there.' I'm trying to have an adventure. I want to tell her I don't want to be mollycoddled. I want to do it all myself. I experience a flush of rebellion, a resurgence of an adolescent emotion that I thought I'd outgrown long ago.

'It's no trouble,' she says kindly, as though responding to a different conversation. 'I'm rostered on duty this weekend, and that includes meeting you. We always meet staff when they come to the Pilbara for the first time, even on Sundays.'

'It sounds as if you do it often.'

'Yes, someone's at the airport almost every weekend. Staff turnover's pretty high. Especially among nurses in remote communities. But I expect you know that already.'

'I wondered. No one actually told me,' I answer, more careful now.

By the time I retrieve my belongings from the luggage carousel and we are outside, the sky has already changed from red to night-navy, speckled with stars. Lights in the parking area blink on as we slam the car doors. It seems only a few minutes' drive in the dark before we pull into a driveway somewhere on the outskirts of the town. The headlights pick out a group of low fibro buildings, all painted khaki. Before long I'll recognise the colour as a government signature. Lights shine through flimsy brown curtains at some of the windows. There's blue flickering from television screens, but the rooms appear empty of humans.

'This is it,' my driver says as she rolls the car to a stop and turns off the engine. 'These places are often vacant, and they use them for people passing through. They're comfortable enough.'

She removes a key from her key ring, checks the number on the yellow tag and indicates the flat in front of us, then hands me the key.

'This is it. Number four,' she says. She gets out and unlocks the boot. 'You must be planning to stay a while. You've brought a lot of gear.'

Together we unload my luggage and put it on the side of the driveway. 'Someone's turned on the porch light to welcome you,' she remarks as she gets back into the car. She leans out of the window.

'Good luck. See you tomorrow.'

I watch her reverse down the driveway. Through the windows, I hear a blast from the car radio before she turns down the volume. She pauses as she reaches the empty street and waves, winds up the window against the heat and dust, and goes back to her interrupted Sunday evening.

Now I'm alone, and discover that it isn't what I wanted after all.

The unit's appearance contradicts my earlier warm welcome. The path and porch by the front door need a thorough sweeping and the frayed coir mat is caked solid with dirt. Cobwebs, laden with dust, festoon the corners of the porch and the windows look as if they haven't been cleaned for years. There is a vaguely unpleasant odour, one I can't identify. It's sweet and burnt and slightly musty.

So much for presentable accommodation, I think. We community nurses pride ourselves on our powers of observation, skills we learn and perfect, that act like little antennae. Clues from the outside environment help us anticipate what might be waiting inside a client's house, thus minimising nasty surprises. Sometimes such surveillance is a matter of our own or others' safety.

My senses warn me about this place.

With a thudding heart, I fumble with the key as I put it into the lock and try to turn it. The lock is stuck and I jiggle the key with growing impatience until it yields. The door has been jammed shut as if the wood has swollen with damp, but that's impossible in the dry heat. I push gently and then with increasing force, but it still doesn't budge. Frustrated, I lean, using my full weight. As the door gives way, I stumble and almost fall across the threshold.

There's a mild flurry in the room, movement I sense rather than see in the dark. There's a strange clicking sound, a noise I can't identify. I grope up and down the wall by the side of the doorjamb for a light switch, not consciously reflecting on the wisdom of confronting whatever is there. When I find it, the plastic switch is sticky. I snap it on.

In the muted light from an unshaded, low-wattage globe that hangs in the middle of the room, I see an army of cockroaches seething across the linoleum and up the walls of a kitchen–living room. These are not the small insects sometimes seen in the south of the state, but larger and more horrifying than any I could have imagined. I stand transfixed for several seconds, just long enough to take in the scene. On wads of newspaper on one of the benches sits a battalion of jam jars decked with prissy gingham mobcaps tied with matching ribbons. Jam runs down the sides of the glass and pools on the newspaper. The gas stove in the corner is covered with burnt jam and cockroaches, and in the sink a large preserving pan sits soaking. Several dead cockroaches float on top of the scummy yellow liquid. Aghast, I escape outside and slam the door behind me.

The curtains in one of the other units twitch, but there is no face at the window. Perhaps I've become hypersensitive to movement? Perhaps I've imagined the cockroaches, too. No one comes out to ask if there's something the matter. My adventure has started to sour. Already, I'm beginning to hate the Pilbara in general and Port Hedland in particular. And since I can't go back into the unit, it's obvious I'll have to find alternative accommodation for the night.

'There's never been a complaint about cockroaches before,' the clerk at the Health Department tells me the next morning. 'And we've had all sorts staying in those flats. Doctors, specialists, scientists.' He pauses and sniffs, an almost imperceptible intake of breath. 'As well as nurses.' He looks up at me over the top of his black-framed glasses. 'None of them ever complained.'

'Perhaps no one else has seen cockroaches like that,' I reply, conscious of the slightly hysterical note in my voice, and wondering if he thinks I've made up the story to get out of staying in the accommodation they provided.

'Those places are supposed to be left clean and tidy,' he grumbles, ignoring my comment. 'There aren't any cleaners.'

I take a deep breath and start again. 'Someone had been making jam,' I say, trying to sound reasonable.

He taps his cheap blue biro on the desk and deliberates. 'No one else has the key to that unit.'

'I just know what I saw.' I feel defeated.

'Anyway,' he goes on, 'I'm not authorised to pay for you to stay in a motel. We aren't made of money.'

'Thinking about those cockroaches makes my stomach churn.'

'You can pay for your motel room yourself, then.'

Later, when I related my cockroach story to the other community health staff in Port Hedland, I would learn that one of the older community nurses regularly used the department's empty flats to make jam and pickles rather than messing up her own place.

There was much that I didn't know about remote area nursing and many things I'd never done. The first morning in Port Hedland I was invited to submit a list of questions that would form the basis of an individual learning program that I'd complete before I could travel to Jigalong. I was clear about some things I'd need to know and guessed about others, but I found it almost impossible to imagine myself at work in an outback nursing post and couldn't realistically predict the gaps in my knowledge or skills.

The inventory I finally generated was random. I imagined that, with no resident doctor, nurses might be expected to do almost anything. At the top of the page I wrote, 'Suturing minor wounds'. I'd never done that. I'd certainly never driven in the outback. The furthest north of Perth I'd been was Geraldton, on four-lane bitumen all the way. I'd avoided driving on gravel roads whenever I could, so I added four-wheel driving over rough terrain to my list, even though I had no idea how rough it would be. I had a smattering of Aboriginal anthropology, but knew I'd work more competently if I had access to culturally specific information about the Martu people who lived at Jigalong, so I included that.

'You can spend several days at the regional hospital,' the Director of Nursing said during a phone call when she got my list. 'The staff will show you enough accident and emergency procedures to get by comfortably.'

I waited for the orientation I needed to unfold, but it didn't happen. Instead, I attended lectures about school health screening, sexually transmitted diseases, diabetes and diet. In the past, I had taught those subjects to other health care professionals. Hospital-trained in the metropolitan area, the only accident and emergency work I'd completed was a compulsory two-month stint during my training. As my first day in the Pilbara progressed, I became increasingly perturbed, unsure what I'd committed to and whether I could deliver what was expected. No one I asked knew if there was a written list of competencies for registered nurses in remote areas. If there was, it seemed they'd never seen it.

'There's another nurse at Jigalong,' one of the supervisors reassured me when I mentioned my apprehension. 'She'll show you everything you need to know. She's got the skills and she'll teach you. There's nothing to worry about.' She handled the pencil on her desk, turning it around thoughtfully before adding, 'She'll be glad when you arrive. She's been on her own for quite a while.'

If I was at all curious about someone working alone in a remote post, I don't remember asking questions, and the woman opposite me volunteered no more information.

I've been sent to observe the work of a child health nurse in her clinic in South Hedland, in a new housing area full of young families. This morning was busy; we visited three new mothers, weighed and measured each tiny baby, and dispensed advice about feeding, sleeping and the care of their older siblings. Now we are trading information while we wait for the first client of the afternoon.

'The Pilbara gets to you after a while,' the nurse says. 'I came here on a working holiday travelling around Australia, fifteen years ago. I met my husband, who worked here. We settled down, built a house we love, had a family. We wouldn't leave for anything.'

'Have you always been a child health specialist?'

'No, only for the past five or six years. I did the postgrad course at Curtin University.'

'Did your family go to Perth with you while you studied?'

'Oh, no. It was only for a year. My husband stayed here and looked after the children. They all came to Perth for the school holidays. And I flew home during the uni breaks.'

'You make it sound easy.'

'It wasn't really. It was a long time to be away from the children. But my husband was wonderful. I'm glad I've done it.'

'I wish I'd done the postgrad course, too.'

'I thought everyone had to have child health qualifications to work in Aboriginal communities?'

'Apparently not. They must know I don't. I sent them a resumé.'

'It'll be pretty difficult without it. It's a big part of the work. Not that I've worked on a community. Too isolated for me. I'm a social person.'

'Everyone says the *real* Jigalong nurse will teach me everything I need to know.'

'Good luck!' she says as the phone rings. She listens for a second, then hands it to me.

'Hello there, Maureen,' a voice greets me. 'We've decided you're ready to go to Jigalong. The community health doctor, Jane, is driving to Newman tomorrow, first thing. You can stay there with her overnight and go on to Jigalong on Thursday when she goes out for the doctor's clinic.'

'Oh. But I don't think I'm —'

'You'll be fine,' she interrupts. 'Jane will pick you up at the motel at six-thirty.'

2

'Look over there,' Jane says, nodding vaguely to the right of the vehicle. 'That's Jigalong. Be quick or you'll miss it.'

Objects glint in the distance as the morning light reflects off roofs or the windows of vehicles. As illusory as the mirages that shimmer in the desert in front of us, Jigalong disappears as suddenly as it had appeared. I'm disappointed; I've been looking forward to this first glimpse for so long. I'd have missed it altogether if Jane hadn't pointed it out, but I wish she'd given me more warning.

Half an hour later, she puts her foot down hard and wrenches the steering wheel. The car lurches out of the deep gully of the wide dry bed of Jigalong Creek, with its fringe of river gums and acacia trees, and the settlement is in full view. There is no welcoming message, not even a signpost to say we've arrived. The track broadens into a graded area as wide as a football field. Colossal tyres from dump trucks used on the mining sites define the edges. They've been splashed with white paint, as if their bulk is not evident enough. Three small, scruffy boys climb on another mound of tyres placed in the middle of the road to slow the traffic entering the settlement. The boys recognise the car and wave.

'Cheeky little buggers,' Jane comments. 'They should be in school.'

To our left, high cyclone-wire fences line the road in front of a series of low buildings, and there are more buildings in the distance ahead of the vehicle. There are a few scrubby bushes and stunted trees, but no grass. A couple of vehicles are parked haphazardly, and several middle-aged black men stand between them, talking and gesticulating energetically.

The day before, we'd made the four-hour trip from Port Hedland to Newman, the closest town to Jigalong. Newman (where Palyku and Wawula countries adjoin) is one of a handful of modern towns scattered sparsely across the vast, iron-rich Pilbara region of Western Australia, which had been purpose-built to serve the mining industry that developed after the discovery in 1957 of a massive iron ore deposit at nearby Mt Whaleback in the Ophthalmia Ranges. By the time I arrived in the Pilbara, Mt Whaleback boasted an open-cut mine said to be the largest in the world, where massive machinery worked day and night, all year round.

I slept the night at Jane's house, billeted in accordance with an outback custom practised by government departments at the time. I'd only ever stayed with family before and was shy about accepting such hospitality from a stranger.

'Thank you for inviting me to stay with you,' I'd said. 'But I'd prefer to go to a motel. I like to be independent.'

'No,' she insisted, 'I have a spare room. You can stay in my house.'

'But I do like my own space.'

'You'll have plenty of that, where you're going. You'll be glad of company after a week.'

In desperation I said, 'It's not what I want.'

'Out here, we don't always get what we want,' she replied. 'Anyway, in return for having a three-bedroom house I provide accommodation for people passing through Newman. Everyone does. It's a way to save money.'

So I spent another restless night, only partly because a streetlight shone onto my pillow through the curtainless window in the spare room. Three days into my adventure as a remote area nurse, and already I was offside with the doctor. Breakfast was a hurried affair, and our conversation stilted.

Five kilometres the other side of Newman, the bitumen gave way to the still-comfortable graded gravel road to Marble Bar, but there wasn't much time to enjoy it before we took a new direction. A pair of faded, bullet-riddled signs pointed towards Balfour Downs Station and Ethel Creek, marking the Jigalong turn-off and the track that heads even further inland into the desert. On the track, we bounced and slewed over washboard corrugations. Soon my hands ached from gripping the seat to avoid being thrown against the roof or smashed against the windscreen.

'This road hasn't been graded since a major flood during the wet season washed most of it away. That was a couple of years ago,' Jane said. 'Not that you can really call it a road.' She concentrated hard to avoid a larger than usual rut. 'No one takes responsibility for it.'

Yesterday we had traversed spectacular terrain between terraced brick red and purple cliffs fringed with massed wildflowers along a new four-lane highway from Port Hedland through the Hamersley Range. Off the Marble Bar road that morning, lavish vistas had given way to stark landscape unbroken by even the hint of a hill. The flat red plains, pocked with termite mounds, stunted mulga and clumps of bristly spinifex, were interspersed with blackened saltpans that would flood in the wet season. Then the road would be impassable.

This gave real meaning to the concept of a country 'where no birds sing', I mused during one of the long silences between us, while Jane negotiated the deep ruts in the track and I meditated on the foolishness of what I'd begun.

On that first trip from Newman I saw no living thing along the way, not even crows feeding on road kill. The only carcasses we passed were those of vehicles abandoned where they'd broken down or been damaged in accidents. Windscreens and windows had been smashed and wheels removed. Station wagons, utilities and pick-up trucks slumped into pools of glass that glittered in the sunlight.

With every kilometre, I felt myself being dragged further from my familiar world into an adventure of seriously risk-taking dimensions.

Two women, one holding a baby over her shoulder, step back as we pull into a driveway. Jane waves vigorously and they wave back. The khaki-painted prefabricated building in front of us squats behind a wire fence, close to the edge of the settlement. A low partition divides the verandah that extends along the front. On one side someone has tried to grow plants in green plastic flowerpots; only the blackened stems remain. I'm relieved to have arrived in one piece after a gruelling ride. I'm more than ready for coffee, and apprehensive about meeting the regular nurse.

'The one closest to the creek is yours,' Jane says, indicating widely with her arm and simultaneously negotiating the vehicle through the narrow gateway. She turns off the ignition and we get out into the heat of the morning. It feels good to stretch the muscles I've held tense for so long.

A wiry woman with short grey hair and weathered skin, dressed in dark knee-length shorts and a blue and white striped shirt, emerges from the door of the larger building next door, where six or seven women and an old man sit on a metal bench in the shade of a verandah.

'That's the clinic,' Jane informs me. 'And here comes Margaret.'

The sensible brown sandals of the approaching woman kick delicate puffs of dust with every step. She wipes her hands on a paper towel as she strides across the compound and through the open gate in the cyclone-wire fence that separates the nurses' flats from the clinic.

'Hello, there,' she says, smiling. She extends a cold, still-damp hand. 'Welcome to Jigalong.'

'This is our resident nurse *extraordinaire*. You've been here forever, haven't you, Margaret?' Jane asks the woman. Then she turns to me and says, 'She'll set you on the right track.' She gives the other woman's arm a quick pat. 'Busy clinic?'

Margaret nods. 'There's a bit of a queue.'

'I'll just help our new nurse put her things inside, and I'll be right with you,' Jane announces.

'You might like to unpack, make yourself at home, Maureen,' Margaret suggests. 'Come over when you're ready. Don't hurry.'

Jane helps me put my bags and boxes in the middle of the floor of a modest room that doubles as sitting and dining space, with a tiny kitchen at one end.

'What a lot of stuff,' she says, running her eyes curiously over the things I've brought with me. Everything looks desolate, covered with dust from the journey. There's a large suitcase full of clothes, the sewing machine I plan to use during what I imagine will be long, lonely evenings, a couple of boxes of books and the bags of groceries I bought yesterday afternoon, when she had gone to work at the community health office in Newman. I don't pretend to be an experienced traveller, and I've carted what I think are the essential props from my suburban life.

'See you later,' she says with one final glance at my possessions as she disappears towards the clinic, leaving me alone to survey the place.

Seeing my bags and boxes on the tobacco-coloured carpet, covered with the gritty particles that will soon be as familiar as a witch's cat, I panic. What if my critics and friends were right when they advised me to stay home and be sensible, to grow old gracefully and live like a respectable grandmother?

I unpack quickly and put almost everything into the built-in cupboards, hoping that if I create even a tiny area of order in my life the surges of panic will recede. I make my bed with the linen I've brought from home, not for a minute imagining that within a couple of weeks they'll be blotched with powdery dust that has stained the fibres of the fabric in a variety of pinks and browns.

I take a pile of folded white shirts from my case and hang them on coat hangers next to my uniform culottes. By the end of the first week I'll have put the lot in a cardboard box on the clinic verandah. They'll be snapped up by some middle-aged Martu women, visitors to the clinic, who will wear them for a day or two before discarding them; I'll have followed Margaret's lead and adopted a uniform of shorts and shirts, ordered in dark colours that will not show the dirt, and brought from Newman to the settlement on the store truck. They'll be just right for squatting or sitting on the ground while I talk with people, and for climbing in and out of the Nissan Patrol that will become my second office.

This one-bedroom flat is nothing like my pretty townhouse with its climbing roses and pink carpets across the road from Kings Park, halfway between Perth and Subiaco, within easy walking distance of both. This Jigalong flat is studiously monochrome; the carpet, tiles, curtains and furniture are all shades of brown. The furniture is sparse and utilitarian. A thin film of dust covers the lot. With a dampened dishcloth from the kitchen I wipe the hard surfaces. The cloth leaves streaky trails — stains I won't be able to erase. It will take more than the few things I've brought to turn this place into a home. There's nowhere to put my books, so I leave them in their boxes, pushed into a corner. There's no coffee table, either. Perhaps I could put a tablecloth over one of the boxes and use that. It will do nicely.

The air in here is cold; Margaret has turned on the air-conditioner ready for me. It's set high on the wall, out of reach.

I climb onto a chair to adjust it and find its only speeds are off and fully engaged. The hum is disconcertingly loud and the skin on my arms has goose bumps. The chilly, confined space unnerves me. I make a cup of instant coffee and take it onto the back verandah to warm up.

Tussocks of spinifex, faded yellow and dull green, grow in the dust in a large backyard complete with a Hills hoist. There are a couple of straggly tamarisk trees near the back fence. Beyond the fence, there's no sign of habitation. Red earth stretches, broken only by spinifex, to a row of low hills in the distance, under the unrelentingly blue sky.

Already the saturated colours of this landscape have become too strong for me, too aggressive. Already I ache for something to soften them: pastels, restful greens and blues and mauves. I recall the hydrangea bushes that grow along the side wall at home. They flower gently in time for Christmas each year, their pink and white flower heads luminous against lush green foliage.

3

Margaret and Jane arrive back at the nurses' quarters before I've seen inside the clinic. I'm vaguely uncomfortable. What if I've been too slow or they think I've been shirking? But it seems the early finish at the clinic has nothing to do with me.

'Some of the Martu wandered away when I came over to meet you,' Margaret explains. 'They'll come back tomorrow. You think you have a busy day ahead, and then it changes without warning. This is one of those times.'

She looks towards the doctor for confirmation, and their eyes meet, excluding me. I sense they have a secret, but try to dismiss the hunch. I hate this paranoid feeling, and I don't know these women well enough to guess what has gone on between them. Refusing Margaret's offer of lunch, Jane is ready to return to town.

'Good luck, both of you,' she calls, waving from her window and spinning the wheels of the vehicle as she reverses from the driveway. 'See you Thursday week.'

'Safe trip,' the nurse calls after the retreating vehicle, but the doctor is already too far away to hear. The car skids sickeningly as she speeds off, but she manages to correct it without hitting anything. We watch until the cloud of dust reaches the creek.

'Most of our clients have a rest in the heat of the day,' Margaret says. 'There's no one over there, but I suppose you're keen to see the clinic?'

'Yes. I'm looking forward to it.'

'It'll be different from anything you've seen,' she warns.

'I'm sure it will. But I want to see where I'll be working for the next few months, or years, even,' I say in what I hope is a neutral tone. In reality, I'd be glad if I could turn around and walk, all the way home.

Margaret leads the way along a short gravel path and through a wire gate with a padlock that I'll soon discover no one uses swinging from its latch. She seems oblivious to the furnace-blast of wind and the heat of the noon-high sun that has sucked all moisture from the air. There's no one sitting on the wooden benches outside the door.

From her pocket, she extracts a key that she's anchored to the waistband of her shorts with a safety pin tied to a length of string. She opens the door with a possessive flourish. Holding the spring-loaded fly-wire screen aside, she ushers me into a combined treatment and waiting room that has not been tidied after the morning's session.

It's impossible to ignore the disarray and difficult not to comment. But Margaret is apparently as unfazed by the mess in here as she was by the heat outside. The sink in one corner is piled high with dirty instruments and dishes with cotton balls floating in cloudy yellow liquid. There's a broken glass on the draining board, within easy reach of a child, and I pick up the fragments. I'm not wearing gloves and I don't use tongs. For the moment, I've forgotten about personal danger.

I look for a sharps box, one of the hard, bright yellow plastic containers with danger signs on each side and on the top. They're meant to be in a prominent place in every treatment room in a health facility. I finally spot one under the jumble on the sink, but I'd have to move too many other things to get to it. I put the glass high on a shelf, hoping I'll remember to dispose of it later. I look at Margaret to see if she's watching, but she's bending over, fiddling with the strap of her sandal, and hasn't noticed.

The once cream-painted walls and woodwork in the clinic are smeared with years of grimy fingerprints. Doors and woodwork need a coat of paint. They're patched with blackened strips from sticky tape where notices have been stuck and fallen off over the years. The dull green vinyl floor is thick with sand that's been carried in on bare feet and not swept away. On the floor in one corner, the stained ticking cover of an old mattress is visible under a rumpled blue sheet. A striped pillow rests on top of two carelessly folded grey army-issue blankets, dumped on the end of the mattress. The walls are lined with chrome and red vinyl chairs. The plastic on several has split open, and grey and yellow foam chips poke through the holes. Finely powdered potato crisps and a red KitKat wrapper lie under one of the chairs.

In an office with minimal equipment, there's an ancient typewriter where I would have expected a computer, and a phone and fax machine. A pile of files, clients' notes by the look of them, have fallen over, spilling pathology reports and other documents onto the desk. Crumpled balls of paper that have missed the bin lie on the floor. In the room Margaret calls the doctor's office, there's an examination table with a soiled, scrunched-up paper sheet. Five used mugs, a tin of cheap instant coffee and a carton of milk stand on the sink in the kitchen. Margaret sniffs the milk, pulls a face, and pours it carefully down the plughole and runs the tap.

'It's gone off,' she comments, sounding surprised. 'Should have put it back in the fridge this morning.'

There are other rooms, but my guide seems suddenly to lose interest in the tour. Back in the office, she begins to straighten the files. They fall over as soon as she takes her hands off them.

'I'm always behind with the paperwork,' she complains. 'There's a lot of work for one person to do, and I mostly enjoy it. But I don't like the writing and filing.'

Loud knocking interrupts us, and she goes to investigate. Seconds later, she puts her head around the door.

'The afternoon stragglers have arrived early. Come into the treatment room. You can see how I deal with things. I'm not expecting too many patients this afternoon. It's usually quiet after Jane's been.'

There's a little procession of people who smile shyly at me; they don't seem to mind that I'm in the room. Margaret introduces each one until I think I'll never be able to remember them all, even though she doesn't use their tribal names. They have minor complaints and I watch as she dispenses headache tablets and cleans a superficial wound that's become infected. She weighs a baby and advises the mother on a new feeding technique because the infant is underweight for her age and length. I'm relieved there's nothing too complicated. What I've seen so far is like being a nurse in a high school and I can do that.

'I was told there were health workers here,' I say when they haven't appeared by mid afternoon. 'When are they on duty?'

'They're both part-timers,' Margaret answers. 'They were here this morning. The doctor needs both of them to interpret. I gave them this afternoon off. You'll meet them when they come tomorrow.'

'Interpret?'

'Yes. English is the third or fourth language for some of the Martu people. They still routinely speak their own languages, not like in many other places. The young ones manage well enough, but the older folk often need an interpreter.'

At the end of the afternoon, sitting on a hard chair by a tiny table with a bright green cloth in Margaret's kitchen, I watch while she takes mugs from the cupboard over the sink and gives them a quick wipe with a stained tea towel. She peers inside to make sure she's removed the dust that has accumulated since she washed them.

The flats are mirror-reversed and share kitchen and bathroom walls and the verandahs. Margaret has lived here for years and, while my space is stark and empty, she's transformed hers from the standard ugly brown to a peaceful haven with framed pictures, colourful cushions, books and ornaments. Her guitar is in a corner near a pile of sheet music on a table. There's more furniture here than in my flat and I notice that some items have been duplicated. Then I realise she's borrowed things from the flat next door when it was vacant. In her position, I might also have decided that itinerant nurses with all their belongings in backpacks needed fewer home comforts than she did, because they'd soon be moving on. I can see I'll have to be creative or make do. I'm certainly not going to ask her to return any furniture.

While the water boils, Margaret produces a carton of long-life skim milk and a packet of chocolate biscuits from the refrigerator.

'To celebrate your arrival,' she says, shaking the biscuits onto a plate. The chocolate has melted at some stage in its journey to Jigalong, and the biscuits have reset in odd, unattractive shapes.

'Looks as if you plan to stay,' she says, leaning against the sink, her back to the window. 'I noticed you've brought a lot of gear.'

My luggage seems to be causing too much comment, and I'm curious.

'I'm not sure how long I'll be here,' I hedge. 'I hope to stay a while. But it depends if I like it and if I can do the work.'

'I'm glad you plan to stay, anyway. So many nurses come and go that I get dizzy. They see it as an adventure, don't take it seriously. The department is so desperate I sometimes think they employ anyone who applies.'

I nod, aware she's describing my situation precisely, but not prepared to admit it.

'Don't get me wrong,' she says. 'Some who come are good at the work — usually those who've worked in hospital emergency departments or operating theatres. That's useful experience for a place like this. But, in the end, it doesn't matter how good they are, they don't stay. It's too isolated, too lonely, too hot. They all have different excuses for leaving.'

She pauses and concentrates as she pours boiling water from the kettle onto the instant coffee in the mugs. She holds up the milk carton and, when I nod, splashes a liberal amount into one mug, leaving the other black.

'One year we had twelve new nurses,' she continues, placing the mugs on the table. She pulls out the chair and sits opposite me. 'That's a lot of people to get to know. It's not good for the community, either, that lack of continuity. Must have given the hierarchy in Hedland a headache, too. They always complain about how hard it is to staff the remote clinics. But the record goes to a place further north, where they had seventeen new nurses in twelve months.' She breaks off a piece of biscuit and pops it in her mouth, then wipes melted chocolate off her fingers with a tissue from the box on the table. 'Anyway, that's not my problem. They're lucky to have the half a dozen or so of us who stay put. I've been here ten years. Before that I worked in a place in the Kimberley region.'

'Why did you leave?'

'There was some bother in the community. I don't like to talk about it.'

'You seem to enjoy it here.'

'Jigalong's all right. There's not too much trouble most of the time, and I love the people and the freedom. This is home for me.'

'I've never lived away from Perth,' I say. I feel shy.

'Really?'

'No. I had a big family. No husband to support us.'

'Like me. But I've only got two kids. They're grown up now.'

'Yes, so are mine.'

'You'll get the hang of being here. It'll take a while.'

'I don't feel quite ready yet.'

'No one does when they first get here. Last year there was a new nurse. He came with the doctor, like everyone else. Anyway, this fellow took one look at the place from the front fence. Jane told me she could see him freeze in his seat. After a minute, he said: "Fuck!" He hardly said another word to anyone. The next morning, he hitched a ride out. No one's seen him since. But like I said, I'm glad you want to give it a go.'

She pushes the plate of biscuits towards me and I bite into a lump of chocolate. There's a long pause.

'That brings me to something you should know,' she says at last. I wait. I hear the intake of air as she draws a deep breath like a radio newsreader getting ready to enunciate an unpronounceable name.

'I'm off to Melbourne on Saturday.'

'Saturday!' I echo stupidly, and immediately inhale biscuit crumbs and start to cough. I splutter and try to catch my breath. Margaret goes to the tap, fills a glass, and gives it to me. The water is tepid and I don't know where it has come from or how clean it is. I've managed to drink only boiled water in the few hours I've been here, planning to check out the purity of the water source as soon as I can. I sip from the glass in my hand anyway.

'That's in two days' time,' I say, when I've recovered. I'm embarrassed. I've been trying hard to impress this new colleague with my confidence. My undignified display won't have helped with that impression.

'One full day and two nights,' she says.

'Who'll replace you?' I ask.

'I've been hanging on until you got here,' she says carefully, intent on stirring the coffee she's already stirred once. 'My annual leave's six months overdue. I've been here by myself for the last four, without a break.'

'Nobody told me you weren't going to be here.' I hear the whimper in my voice, or perhaps it's rising panic.

'Nobody knew. I almost made up my mind yesterday. But I decided definitely after I chatted with Jane this morning. I rang Port Hedland and told them while you were unpacking.'

That could explain the doctor's rapid departure without stopping for lunch, leaving us alone so the woman opposite me could break the news.

'What about the community? Won't they mind?'

'You are a registered nurse?' she counters with a question of her own, with the slightest emphasis on 'registered'.

'Yes.'

'There shouldn't be a problem, then. As long as there's a nurse here, the Martu people don't care who it is. I need a holiday.'

I wonder why she hasn't had a holiday for so long. *My* contract with the Health Department says nurses are entitled to seven days' leave, with a return airfare to Perth, after every three months' work. That's as well as six weeks' annual leave, and extra days for public holidays. Perhaps Margaret's so devoted to the job she didn't want to go away until now. Or maybe she has nowhere to go. Somehow, this doesn't seem the right time to ask.

'There's a remote area nurses' conference in Melbourne next week,' she says, 'and now you're here, it's the perfect opportunity for me to go. It'll be good to catch up with other old-timers. We come from all over Australia. Some of us have been around for years. We have lots in common and there are always new stories to swap. Oh, yes. And there's the conference. Mustn't forget the formal part,' she laughs.

I make a little noise, a kind of gurgle that I try to suppress; it sounds as if I'm being strangled. But apparently the other woman takes it to mean I'm encouraging her to go on talking.

'One of my sons is getting married, the week after the

conference as it turns out. I hadn't planned to go — I thought it'd be too hard to arrange. But they'll all be thrilled if I turn up. I'll visit other family and friends, too. I've got plenty of places to stay down south. I should be back in four weeks or so.'

She pauses again and crosses her arms on her chest. It's a defensive gesture. She must notice the distressed expression on my face, because she softens slightly and says: 'Sorry. I'm off. On Saturday.' She sits back in her chair, no doubt feeling relieved now she's told me. 'There's plenty of time. I'll show you the ropes, introduce you around.' She smiles, softens further. 'You'll be all right. And the health workers know everyone. They're competent. They'll help.'

She stands and begins to tidy away the coffee things.

'I'll do the on-call duty tonight and tomorrow,' she says as I get up to leave. 'You'll have enough of it when I'm gone.'

'Thanks,' I say, not understanding what she's talking about. 'See you tomorrow.'

Next door in my own flat, I throw myself on the bed, hoping Margaret's words will stop hammering in my head. In spite of a stern directive to give myself time to calm down, the self-doubt that has smouldered somewhere just out of my consciousness flares. I want to cry. I want to hide. I want to run away.

I'm an impostor, I think. I can't suture wounds or insert intravenous catheters. I've never had to use the resuscitation techniques we learned in hospital wards where the equipment was up to date and accessible. And now, without warning, I'm to be abandoned in this basic nursing post in unfamiliar territory, almost before I've arrived. I've been told I'll be doing the work of two nurses for a month. It's like walking onto the stage in front of a live audience to perform in a play I haven't even read, and someone's directing me to take both the leading roles. I've been given no opportunity to refuse or even to learn the parts.

It's different for Margaret, I reflect in a surge of self-pity. She's had years of experience. If I was fair, I'd acknowledge she's been alone for months and I will only be here by myself for one. But she knows what she's doing. That's the important difference. I imagine she speaks the local Martu Wangka language at least well enough to get by. I'd assumed everyone here would speak English until she told me otherwise.

I'd like to believe her assurances that I can do the work, but an inventory of my skills would quickly expose my many weaknesses. Legally, I'm obliged to work within my competency or under supervision until I'm proficient, but soon I'll be pushed far beyond my capabilities. I know already that coming to Jigalong is the worst mistake I've ever made. By accepting the job, I've demonstrated ignorance and arrogance. I shouldn't have come, even as the back-up nurse. Now I'm trapped.

The pulse in my temple beats against the pillow, and a tiny nerve in the corner of my eyelid pulsates, too. I roll over with my back to the window and put a pillow over my head. It blocks out the hideous redness of the sunset through the window. This is another, stronger, version of my first miserable evening in the Pilbara.

4

It's dark. I've been asleep and in my absence night has fallen. I lie still on this strange bed in an unfamiliar room, trying to remember where I am. The desert, that's where, I recall, and my heart crumbles under the weight of the memory. In just two days I'll be here alone with more responsibility than I can endure.

Sitting up slowly, I reach for the bedside light. The room is cell-like and the bed is jammed against the wall, but even so there's barely enough room to walk to the wardrobe or the door. There's a phone on the bedside table. It's an odd place to put the only phone; the living room would have been more convenient. But already I'm past wondering why things happen the way they do at Jigalong.

Perched on the edge of the bed, I dial a familiar number. I've been warned that personal calls must be strictly limited to emergencies, but I think my predicament is more a crisis than an emergency, so a call to the outside world is amply justified. I count as the phone rings, and picture Rosemary Keenan's living room, where the phone is on the desk near the door.

Rosemary can be trusted to shore up my faltering confidence. Over the years, what began as a working relationship has blossomed into the kind of respectful friendship that allows us to say what we think, which is not always what the other wants to hear. I will her to pick up the phone, anxious to hear her familiar greeting. I'll be distressed if I'm connected to the answering machine. I'll hang up if she's not there.

'I can't do this,' I wail as soon as she answers. 'I'm really glad you're there.'

'So am I,' she replies.

'I've just been told I'm going to be here by myself for a month. Starting first thing on Saturday. I'm terrified,' I blurt out.

'You're not! How did that happen? That's scary. It'd terrify anyone.' I'm gratified by her reaction.

'I don't have the skills to do accident and emergency stuff,' I say.

'No,' she says. 'But registered nurses can do anything.'

'That's not funny. Be serious. What can I do? Help! The nurse who's leaving won't have time to hand over properly. A week wouldn't be enough, even if I had the basic experience.'

'Would it help to talk about what frightens you most?'

'It might,' I say doubtfully.

'What's the worst thing that could happen?' Her no-nonsense voice is that of a senior nurse with a probationer.

'A breech birth,' I say without hesitation. 'At three o'clock in the morning. In a blackout.' I haven't given any shape to specific disasters up until now. Instead, my fear has been amorphous, an all-pervading dense fog. 'A breech birth in broad daylight would be difficult. But a woman experiencing a complicated birth by torchlight, with me as the only midwife, would be a disaster. For everyone.'

'Mmm. That would be bad. What else?'

'Almost everything . . .'

'On second thoughts, don't let's go there,' Rosemary interrupts. 'It was a silly question to ask someone who's already freaking out.'

I'd prefer it if she'd told me some untruths, like nothing bad could happen. But the reality is that it can and, as we both know, probably will. She could tell me I'll handle everything well. But, of course, I won't.

'Listen,' she says. I wait, hoping she'll say the only solution is for me to go into Newman and get on a plane to go home tomorrow. 'You're stuck there,' she says. There's a pause and I imagine her trying to find something comforting to say.

'Understatement!'

'At least temporarily,' she goes on, ignoring my interruption. There's another long pause. I'm optimistic she'll find a way to normalise this bizarre situation. She doesn't disappoint me.

'I expect you know more about health care and nursing and managing medical crises than most of the people at Jigalong,' she tells me.

'That might be true, even if what I know doesn't seem like much. What I don't know outweighs —'

'Being negative isn't helpful.'

'No ...'

'You'll just have to fake it,' she says, after another long pause. 'Until you make it. Yes, that's it! You'll have to pretend you can do it.'

'That's dishonest.'

'Probably,' she concedes. 'Do you have a better idea?'

Rosemary's pragmatism steadies me and I begin a new inventory of my abilities, telling myself a story different from the one full of incompetence and fear that I've conjured up since Margaret announced she was going away. I've always experienced the start of a new job as stressful, but I also know that in the past I've quickly warmed to unfamiliar roles and adapted to new circumstances. Faking it until I make it will be no different from the pretending I've done before in new situations. Probably like everyone else, I've done it many times.

'Remember the first time you wore a veil, and went on duty in a ward as a registered nurse?' Rosemary asks.

I have a flash of memory.

After three years in a hospital apprenticeship system, when we'd learned the basics of what our tutors called 'the art and science of nursing', and we had finally qualified for registration with the Nurses' Board, my class was issued with the uniforms of staff nurses. We'd no longer wear white aprons, stiffly starched belts and little caps perched on our heads at whatever rakish angle we could achieve without censure. Instead, we'd wear plain blue dresses for the twelve months it would take to prove we were worthy to wear the sisters' white.

In the nurses' home, we daubed unwieldy squares of muslin with cold-water starch, and painstakingly ironed the fabric dry without scorching it. After three or four applications of starch and repeated ironing, the muslin became stiff enough to be folded in the prescribed fly-away shape that could be worn as a veil — a signifier of our new status. Borrowed from the habits of religious women, together with the title 'Sister', these monstrosities were remnants from nineteenth-century tradition, when good nurses were expected also to be subservient women. The uniform, veil and title denoted a registered nurse's place in the hospital's hierarchy.

It took a week or two before I felt comfortable wearing a veil, tortuously anchored to my head with strips of gauze and an arsenal of pins, and to accept the responsibilities and privileges that went with it. By the time I'd forgotten about my veil and could negotiate doorways and bed frames without knocking it sideways, I was also wearing the authority of a registered nurse as if I'd always been one.

I put down the receiver feeling less trapped. Of course I can do it! I've been told the Aboriginal health workers are capable. I will rely on them. There are other professionals to consult, doctors and nurses, at the end of the phone line which, Margaret told me, had only recently been extended to Jigalong. Before that, all communication was by radio, beamed through the Royal Flying Doctor Service in Port Hedland. Being here would have been much more difficult a couple of years ago.

I go to the boxes in the sitting room and delve into them until I unearth the books I'm looking for. On top is the weighty tome on physiopathology I'd bought in Perth before I left. It's hard to believe it was less than a week ago. Next, there's a well-thumbed general nursing text, followed by my faithful old midwifery bible stuck together with sticky tape, a community health reference, and a little book about working with Aboriginal people, written by a social work lecturer. There's a copy of Robert Tonkinson's *The Jigalong Mob: Aboriginal Victors of the Desert Crusade*, the result of his research from when he lived here in the 1960s. It will, I think, furnish much needed background information and the history of the Martu people. I set the books up on top of one of the boxes, in pride of place in the sitting room.

This library will be my talisman. Instead of panicking and running away, I'll stand my ground like the adventurer I claim I am, and see what happens next.

5

'I thought I'd get a head start and finish everything before I leave on Saturday,' my colleague greets me when I arrive at the clinic the next morning. She waves vaguely at the files on the desk in front of her and an in-tray full of pathology and X-ray reports. 'You can run the morning clinic. It's a good way to learn, and you can ask me about anything you don't know. One of the health workers will be here soon.'

It's too early for clients yet, and I open and shut the cupboards in the treatment room, methodically noting where each piece of equipment is stored. Being able to find everything quickly will save time, and in an emergency could even save a life.

I've scarcely begun my inventory before a plump Martu woman with a pleasant smile appears at the door. She's dressed in a floral skirt and a dark blue T-shirt with the words RESPECT YOURSELF emblazoned across her ample bosom in red and white lettering. It's the logo of a health campaign recently developed by the Drug and Alcohol Authority in Perth.

'Hello, Sister,' she greets me. 'I'm Joannie, one of the health workers.' Her voice is warm, her words softly burred.

'Hello,' I reply. 'My name's Maureen. I don't like being called Sister. I'd much prefer Maureen.' Her handshake is firm, reassuring. 'I'm looking forward to working with you,' I add.

'Yes,' she says in a noncommittal voice. 'Is Margaret here, Sis ...?'

'She's in the office.'

She wanders off to find Margaret and I can hear them talking in low voices in the next room. When she returns, she spreads a blue bedsheet over a trolley and sets out a collection of bowls, instruments and lotions.

'These are the things we'll need today,' she explains as she works.

This must be how she's been taught to do it, I think. It may be efficient, but I prefer to treat each patient separately, setting up and cleaning as I go. I don't say anything. I'll be able to do things my way soon enough.

Joannie introduces the patients as they come through the door. Like yesterday, their complaints are minor; there's nothing complicated, nothing I can't handle easily. By morning teatime, when Margaret joins us, I'm already feeling more confident.

'I told you you'd be fine,' she says.

'Yes, but this is routine. I'm not sure about emergencies,' I start, but it seems prudent not to go any further. There's no point, especially now I've decided I'm going to do the work. She disappears into the office and closes the door again, leaving Joannie and me to deal with the clients. There's a steady stream for the rest of the morning. It continues, after an extended lunch break, well into the afternoon.

We're about to close when a Martu man who seems to be looking for someone puts his head around the door. When he sees only Margaret, Joannie and me he slides his sturdy frame into the room. His age is indeterminate, though he's probably in his late thirties. His jeans and T-shirt are stained and his feet bare. A headband partly tames his unruly hair. When he comes closer, I'm disappointed to find that the band is plaited from red knitting wool, and not woven from some traditional material as I first thought.

'This is PW, the other health worker,' Margaret introduces him. She turns to him before he has time to greet me, and asks: 'You've been away?'

33

'Been in Hedland, eh,' he replies good-naturedly. 'Busy time there.'

'You're always off somewhere,' she comments. 'Did you take your wife and the kids with you?'

'Not this time,' he says. 'Too much business, eh.'

'Just as well you only work part time. And just as well you and Joannie stand in for each other, too. It means you can have a lot of time off.'

'Yo,' the man agrees with a happy grin.

Margaret has invited some other residents to share a barbecue meal before she leaves. She says she wants them to meet me, but I can see the party is as much to farewell her as anything. There are eight or ten of us, all Caucasians.

'There should have been more, but the teachers are away for the school holidays,' our hostess tells me. 'The health workers were invited, too, but they don't often accept my invitations.'

I work hard to memorise people's names and occupations, but before I'll have an opportunity to demonstrate my memory skills half of them will have moved on.

Members of a transient population that came and went continually, new arrivals had their own, often complex, reasons for being in the settlement, including altruism, the lure of money or the need to escape from some impossible situation elsewhere. Some, like me, were stretching their boundaries, seeking an adventure.

Coordinators, nurses, teachers, project officers, storekeepers, tradespeople and accountants forged links between the community and the numerous government agencies involved with the settlement. With few exceptions — of which my nursing colleague was one — outsiders stayed a day, a month or, at most, a couple of years, and when they felt the time was right or when they could no longer stand the isolation, flies and heat, they left. Departures were often abrupt. I suspect the majority of us left nothing behind, not even memories in the minds of the Martu people, while our own experiences would be interludes that would significantly alter our lives forever.

When we've cooked our steaks and sausages and eaten them with bread and butter — there were no salad vegetables in the store today — we move inside, out of the gusting wind. Margaret asks, 'Anyone want coffee?'

A couple of people groan and then one or two say, 'Yes, please.'

'We're sick of drinking coffee, but it's against the by-laws to bring alcohol into the settlement,' someone tells me. 'The community is determined to prevent drunkenness that leads to disorderly or violent behaviour. The no-alcohol rule works pretty well, most of the time, too.'

'So don't get caught bringing grog in,' someone adds. 'That's a no-no.'

'Thank goodness it won't bother me,' I say with a laugh. 'And I don't smoke, either!'

'We all have to be sober to deal with emergencies and light the runway if we need to, anyway.'

'Has Margaret told you about the Royal Flying Doctor Service emergency flights, Maureen?'

'Only that they happen occasionally.'

'Yeah, well — that's what we all hope!'

'Anyway, it'll be something for you to look forward to. An RFDS callout at night is a real experience.'

'Oh, come on now. Don't let's frighten the new nurse before she's even started.'

6

I watch from the front verandah as Margaret throws her swag into the tray of her utility, followed by an overnight bag and an esky. She pulls a black vinyl cover over the lot and buckles it firmly, yanking here and there along the sides to make sure it's secure. She's clearly excited to be heading south to destinations that will be wetter and greener than Jigalong.

I'm ready to concede that she deserves her holiday and recognise it's churlish to wish she was staying, even though I have no idea what to expect in the month ahead, and not knowing renders me powerless with apprehension. I'm determined she won't see how I feel, so I wave and smile enthusiastically as she reverses down the driveway.

When her ute is out of sight, I put on the wide-brimmed hat that I hung on a nail that I found by the back door when I unpacked, and venture out. It's the first time I've been beyond the health compound and I feel vulnerable. Off the verandah, I'm immediately aware of the strange harshness of the country, the dry heat, the flaring sunshine. Although I have a formal role and work here and I've met a few people briefly, no one knows me. I'm a stranger who must wait and hope I'll be accepted. Tingling with trepidation, I wander towards the centre of the settlement where a hodgepodge of shacks and huts sprawls in the dust, interspersed with a more conventional house or two.

The early colonists did not rush to inhabit this part of the Pilbara. The blistering summer heat and scanty rainfall made the place inhospitable for white settlers, and there was no reliable pasture to graze cattle or sheep. Aboriginal people who lived nearer the coast to the west of the desert brought news to the locals of white settlement. They also came with Western goods to trade during the occasional ceremonial and other meetings that brought the groups together.

In time, desert-dwelling Aboriginal people also made contact with the settlers. Some of the men were encouraged to labour as station hands and stockmen on newly established pastoral stations; women were employed to do domestic work in the homesteads. Instead of regular pay, the workers were given commodities like sugar, tea, flour and tobacco, and occasional handouts of meat when stock animals were slaughtered. Because there were so few white women, Aboriginal women were sometimes sexually exploited by the white men.

Early immigrants had taken rabbits to south-eastern Australia, hoping to breed them for food, but the rabbits escaped and multiplied until they reached plague proportions, destroying crops wherever they spread. The government, afraid the pests would cause havoc if they reached Western Australia, constructed what became known as the No. 1 Rabbit-Proof Fence in an attempt to prevent them reaching the more settled areas. The fence started at Starvation Harbour, just west of Esperance on the south coast, and stretched to Cape Keraudren on the north-west coast south of Broome.

Maintenance depots were built at intervals along the continuous 1139-mile (1833-kilometre) fence, said to be the longest in the world. One depot was built in 1907 at Jigalong, in the south-east corner of Palyku country. The depot became a camel-breeding centre, raising and training camels to ride and for use as pack animals by the boundary riders who mended the fence and kept it in good order. Government employees staffed the depot and encouraged Aboriginal men to work for them for handouts.

Loss of independence was a gradual process for the desert people who came from several nearby countries and language groups. Encouraged by the government, the superintendent of the depot became responsible for distributing rations to people who settled nearby, creating a stable food supply which may have been appealing to hunters and gatherers in a harsh climate.

Two years before the depot was set up, the Aborigines Act (1905) had established the position of Chief Protector as the legal guardian of all Aboriginal children in Western Australia. Children could be removed forcibly from their parents and taken to live in missions and orphanages. In addition, under the Act, Aboriginal people could be moved, without consultation or their permission, from one area of the state to another.

The futility of the rabbit-proof fence as a barrier eventually became obvious. Rabbits continued their movement west through holes in the wire and gates left open, and under the fence where trees roots had eroded the soil. Forty years after the construction of the depot at Jigalong, the government encouraged the Apostolic Church of Australia to replace it with a mission. The mission was later re-established about ten kilometres away from the original depot, on a site with a more reliable water supply.

By co-opting and subsidising church and other welfare organisations to distribute rations and provide education and health care for Aboriginal people in rural and remote areas, the government minimised the cost to itself of providing these services. In return, the churches obtained funding and the opportunity to proselytise among the local people. While this arrangement served the interests of the state and church, it was disastrous for the Aboriginal people.

The missionaries at Jigalong did not recognise the deeply spiritual foundation of Aboriginal life. They had no concept of the richness of customary law and traditions and little respect for the people, their kinship system, their relationship to the land, or their culture. The missionaries set up a school, provided health care and doled out subsistence rations to the adults. Children were coerced to the mission in the hope that they could be converted to Christianity. Girls and boys, brothers and sisters, were separated from their parents and from each other. At night the children were locked in segregated dormitories and during the day they attended the school where no one spoke their languages. Their parents camped on the far side of the creek, but the children were forbidden to visit.

The mission workers established the Jigalong Pastoral Station and a labour pool for other stations in the region. There was frequent conflict between the graziers and missionaries about the use of tobacco and alcohol, and the graziers' sexual relationships with Aboriginal women.

In 1967, the mission withdrew. It had failed dismally in its attempts to convert the people of Jigalong to Christianity. As it had done with the mission, the government again minimised its financial responsibility for administration of the settlement by delegating it to the community. Lacking the sophisticated skills they needed to interact with the wider Australian society or to meet the demands for accountability imposed on them, the Martu people found it difficult to administer social security payments and injections of additional funds from the new federal Labor government. The imposed money economy did not sit comfortably with a community in which social organisation was based on kinship obligations and the communal sharing of resources. The transfer of management created enormous problems. Everyone expected enough money to satisfy their needs; the more vocal demanded enough to satisfy their newly discovered wants. Kinsfolk disagreed over the purchase and use of vehicles and other goods.

Government officials, frustrated with what they saw as the inability of the people to manage their affairs, insisted that the community should become incorporated as a legal entity to create an organisation accountable and liable for the funds it received. Incorporation enabled the community to employ staff from outside — almost all of them non-Indigenous — who could manage well enough to comply with the government's demands.

The residents elected a council to oversee the new Jigalong Community Incorporated, but the council, too, was beset by difficulties. The leaders were expected to deal with a multitude of government agencies, all with their own range of different needs and expectations, as well as solve internal problems in the settlement. Leadership changed often as the result of disagreements over favours given and received. Understandably, people were unwilling to hold positions that were seen in a negative light by their kinsfolk, or likely to damage their relationships and reputations because of unpopular decision-making.

The area outside the protective wire fence of the health compound is strewn with detritus, the accumulation of years. Plastic bags cling to the fences; broken glass and intact empty bottles, rusting cans, cardboard cartons, desiccated bones and piles of discarded clothing litter the ground. Sheets of paper move languidly in the hot wind.

This doesn't fit with what I've heard about the relationship of Aboriginal people and their country. What could explain such volumes of rubbish strewn everywhere, if the land has significance and worth that originates from the Law? I wonder.

One explanation might be that the presence of white settlers and missionaries, the imposition of a colonial culture and the materialism of the twentieth century, have worked together to defile Jigalong. Maybe, I ponder, trying to make sense of what I see, the settlement has been excised from country by some process that I don't understand.

Later, when I've had time to think about it, I decide that this is an anomalous piece of ground, neither one thing nor another, an area that no longer belongs exclusively to Aboriginal culture nor yet to white culture, but which bears the burdens of both, much as a cemetery bears liability for the burial of corpses and, at the same time, supports the hopeful rituals and memorials of the living. It is Aboriginal land; it is also the site of an invasion, not with guns and poison, but with mostly good intentions and Bibles.

Halfway between the clinic and the store, set well back from the road, the school is an island in the sea of rubbish. It looks like many of the metropolitan schools I've worked in, with its neatly fenced green grass and conventional playground equipment shaded by exotic trees. Although it's Saturday, some girls aged about nine or ten years old sit by the side of the road outside the padlocked gate. They do not look at me, but appear to be examining the ground in front of them.

'Hello,' I say as I walk past. They don't seem to hear me, and no one answers. I'm not sure whether to repeat myself and decide against it.

Soon I hear them behind me, giggling and chattering in a language I've never heard. I stand still on the roadway until they catch up.

'You're the new sister,' one of the girls says shyly, looking at her feet.

'That's right. Sister or nurse. I like to be called "Nurse" best.'

'Sis,' they respond like a well-trained choir. I start walking again and the girls fall into step around me. The giggling

41

resumes, muffled hisses and spurts of sound that soon become irrepressible laughter.

'Did I say something funny?' I ask. I'm embarrassed, aware of my difference and gaucheness. I might be new to the settlement, but new nurses are not a novelty. The children's laughter seems personal and I'm affronted. My anxiety escalates. It takes a long time for one of them to answer; they go on talking among themselves as if I wasn't there.

Fake it until you make it, I remind myself. Fake being calm and you'll become calm.

'Funny hat. Man's boots,' says the bravest of the girls, pointing at my sneakers. 'That's what mans wear.'

I'm mortified by her frank assessment of my clothing, which seems sensible and practical to me. I can't think of a reply, so walk on in silence, now flanked by the girls.

'I'm going to the store,' I volunteer after a minute or two. 'Can you show me where it is, please?'

'There!' they shout, pointing to the largest building in the settlement.

It is a low, flat structure without windows. A small wooden awning covers the front door and there are wooden seats on either side. There's a heavy concentration of plastic, cartons and cans strewn for twenty metres on either side of the entrance. Inside, it's hot, dark and musty. A meagre selection of fruit and vegetables wilts in a refrigerated cabinet. There is an abundance of junk food full of sugar, salt and fat, and short on nutrients. The groceries, cleaning products and hardware are arranged sparsely on the shelves, as if the building was meant for a more important enterprise and someone has decided to spread the stock out to fill the available space. There are no shopping trolleys lined up outside. Everyone here, I will soon learn, shops for their immediate needs. There are only a dozen refrigerators in the whole settlement; the Martu people do not store food for later.

At the back wall, I examine the meat in the deep freeze until I find a packet of chicken. Several pairs of eyes examine me covertly from under half-closed lids. I'm under scrutiny, a stranger in this tight-knit community where ties of blood or kinship relate everyone. I'm determined not to give in to the apprehension that's causing my palms to sweat. Instead, I saunter slowly towards the front door, casually inspecting items on the shelves as I go.

An old, stooped woman walks nonchalantly through the checkout. She's wearing three or four skirts; they pad her thin hips and hang in grubby layers above her skinny ankles and bare, calloused feet. The worker standing at the cash register shouts and the old woman's mouth distorts in a toothless smile as she turns in response.

'Hey, old woman! Come back here. You can't walk off with that. You gotta pay. You can't walk through like that!' The worker's voice increases in pitch and volume with every syllable. She takes her responsibility for the store very seriously.

The old woman looks at the source of all the noise. It's clear she doesn't understand a word that's being said, but her shoulders droop and she shuffles her feet. She's become the centre of attention for a group that's gathering to enjoy the spectacle. A bystander says something in language and the old woman laughs.

'Look at 'er. Pockets full o' things pinched from shelves,' the woman at the checkout appeals to the audience. 'Someone better stop 'er.'

'I watch 'er takin' stuff,' volunteers a customer who's waiting to go through the checkout.

'Why didn't you stop 'er then? No good lettin' 'er go.'

The old woman speaks volubly, pulling faces and waving her free arm angrily. She pushes back into the store, past a toddler who falls into a display of potato chips. The woman and child trample over the packets on the floor as they scramble to regain their footing. A couple of youths step forward, but don't seem to know what to do next and fall back with their arms by their sides.

A door opens and a man comes out of the office and stands in the old woman's way, blocking the door to the outside. I recognise him from Margaret's barbecue. The woman throws the groceries onto the floor at his feet, still yelling. He steps to one side and lets her go. The crowd cheers and disperses.

'Good morning, Maureen,' he greets me. 'You're up early after last night.'

'So are you, Ian,' I counter.

'It's part of my job as the community accountant to manage the store, so I'm here early most mornings,' he explains. 'Has your boss gone, then?' I hadn't thought of Margaret as my boss, but I don't challenge him.

'Straight after breakfast. She has a very long drive ahead of her.'

'It's not all that bad — only 1700 kilometres. You get used to it when you've done it a few times. Sally and I drive up and down a couple of times a year. We mostly do it in a day, taking turns at driving.'

'That was an interesting introduction to the store,' I say, indicating the old woman who is sitting under a tree outside. 'Poor old thing!'

'Happens all the time. The old folk, you know. They haven't caught up with the twentieth century.' He dismisses the incident with a slight wave. 'Anyway,' he changes the subject, 'Sally and I were wondering when we'd catch up with you again. We live in a house on the other side of the road from the clinic, near the coordinator's. We'll have a coffee or something.'

'That'd be good. Thanks.'

'Got work to do,' he excuses himself as he turns to go back into the office.

'G'day,' the young woman at the cash register says as soon as Ian disappears. 'That old woman. She comes 'ere every day. Thinks she can get away with it.'

'Poor old thing,' I say again, putting my chicken pieces on the counter.

'Nah. She knows. That's one dollar, thanks.'

'A dollar?'

'Yo. Everythin's a dollar.'

'But it's good chicken,' I protest. 'Well within its use-by date.'

'A dollar,' she repeats. 'The same price for everything.'

After a short time, I'd grow accustomed to spending the same amount on an apple or a frozen leg of lamb, or buying a packet of cereal that cost as much as a potato or a block of chocolate, but that morning it was a novel idea. The accounting system was simple for customers and the store's staff. Most of the time, the cost of my basket of groceries, fruit, vegetables and meat balanced out.

For the Martu community, hot pies and sauce, lollies and biscuits, cans of Coca-Cola and ice-creams, consumed at the door, competed with meat and vegetables which required effort to prepare and provided less immediate satisfaction. Any attempts to educate the community about changes to their diet that could bring about long-term benefits for their own and their children's health would end in frustration.

The store seemed to mystify the old people, but after the first few times I saw them accused of shoplifting I wondered what the shouting and agitation were about. Sometimes, it seemed like a game they played. They were always apprehended before they got through the door, their stolen goods returned, and no harm was ever done, except, perhaps, to their pride.

*　　*　　*

Back in the flat, grateful to be out of the sun, I kick off the shoes the little girls found so offensive and sit at the table with a glass of cold water. Before I can open my book, there's a loud knocking on the fly-wire door. Three young women and two toddlers stand on the verandah.

'You very late, Sis,' one of the women reproaches me. 'We watched you go to the store.'

'Oh,' I say. 'I'm sorry. It's Saturday. The clinic isn't open today.'

'Sister Margaret always opens it.'

'She told me she opens on the weekend only if there's an emergency,' I say. 'Is this an emergency?'

'Yes,' they say together.

The hands of the clock above the kitchen window point to nine-thirty. From now until lunchtime I'll be inundated by people claiming they need emergency treatment. They complain of sore fingers, eyes and throats. One has a cough and another sniffles and wheezes. There are sudden attacks of dizziness, abdominal pain and headaches. When the procession dwindles away around midday, I close the door and lean against it, thankful for the respite.

When the second wave begins, with people fresh from their rest knocking on the door of my flat every half-hour or so, I recognise that this is a test. The Martu people want to see how the new nurse measures up.

7

After what's turned out to be a full day's work, I rummage in the cutlery drawer in the flat, searching through an accumulation of plastic and metal gadgets left behind by a succession of nurses who've lived here before me. I'd like to tip the lot out onto the table, discard things that are blunt, rusty or worn out, wash everything else, and replace what's useful in a freshly cleaned drawer. But I don't have time for that now. I have a more urgent task. I shuffle everything impatiently, hating the noise of unfamiliar objects rattling and grating together.

Among the junk, I find a knife I hope will be sturdy enough. I take the frozen chicken from its plastic packaging and, sitting at the table, insert the pointed tip of the knife between two pieces of flesh. They're bonded by solid ice, but I don't want to defrost the lot before I'm ready to use it. I flex the knife backwards and forwards until, using brute strength, I prise off a piece that turns out to be a thigh, complete with baggy, goose-fleshed skin and yellow fat. I put it into a basin on the sink. Even in the air-conditioning, it won't take long to thaw.

While I wait, I make a mug of coffee and take it onto the verandah, where I watch an amazing sunset. The sky is crimson again, but this evening it is possible to distinguish clouds flaring apricot close to the horizon, and to see the evening star. For the first time, I notice how quickly night falls here on the Tropic of Capricorn.

Standing at the kitchen sink, I scoff a TV dinner from the freezer, heated in the microwave oven. I haven't eaten properly for days. I promise myself I'll soon start preparing healthy meals, although it might be quite a challenge, given the ingredients available at the store. Home cooking will certainly be more comforting than packaged, frozen meals.

I'm soon back at the table, impatient to get on with my task. I set out the equipment on the tray that comes with the sterile suturing package that I took, feeling guilty, as if I was stealing, from the pile in the cupboard in the clinic. The green surgical gloves are a size too big and slippery with the talcum powder sprinkled liberally inside before they were wrapped and sterilised ready for use.

There are still a few ice crystals, but they melt as I handle the meat. I hack into it with a paring knife, sawing a deep cut parallel to the bone. It's hard work that hurts my hand. A scalpel would make a cleaner cut and I'll remember to bring one over here next time. When I'm satisfied the gash is deep enough, I set about trying to sew it up again, teaching myself to suture.

I discover that pushing a curved, pre-threaded needle in and out of flesh is not as easy as it looked when I'd watched surgeons at work. As well as a point, the needle has a sharp cutting edge along one side, which cuts a hole in the flesh for the thread to follow, but there's a grating sensation in my fingertips each time I insert the needle. I'm using sterile forceps rather than touching the flesh, which, if this were a real wound, would help prevent the spread of infection.

Inserting the sutures isn't impossible, but tying the knots is beyond me. Anyone who's tried to tie a knot in synthetic thread, using tweezers in one hand and pliers in the other, will have an idea of the degree of dexterity it demands. After a dozen attempts, I decide that the sterile gloves will have to be enough protection against infection. Rather than use the instruments, I tie off each suture with my fingers, using the best reef knots I can execute.

Needlework and embroidery were considered essential elements of a rounded education for young ladies in my school days. Sister Mary St Theophane taught us to sew as routinely as she taught us English, Latin, French, maths and history. She believed her girls were capable of anything, but even she would have been amazed to see me at work. Customarily dextrous with needle and cotton, I find suturing flesh with catgut more difficult than any sewing task I've ever attempted. But, now I've accepted the challenge, it's a great deal more fun than inserting dainty stitches into pre-printed linen doilies for the school fete.

Over the next few days, I practised suturing different cuts of meat, experimenting with a range of textures until I could do the task easily. When I was reasonably adroit, I relaxed. But I would soon find that sewing lumps of inanimate flesh was a poor imitation of suturing lacerations on children and adults without the benefit of even local anaesthetic. My first authentic experience was when I sutured the foot of a little girl with a heavily bleeding gash, caused by jumping on a broken bottle. After that first time, suturing became one more skill to be used, repeatedly and, eventually, almost casually.

I sutured wounds from scalps to the soles of feet. Some of the lacerations were horrific, but my competence improved and my confidence soared with each one. My suture-lines were effective, administered with a minimum of commotion, and conducive to healing, even if no one would ever be able to claim that their scar was the handiwork of a plastic surgeon.

8

The rest of the first week passed in a blur of panic and discomfort. When I try to recall details, I can conjure up only fuzzy, confused images and a sense of desperation from the lack of sleep. Cut off from my ordinary life, what I saw seemed to have nothing to do with what I knew or who I'd been. Unimagined sights, sounds and smells assaulted my senses. My own behaviour, which I'd once considered polite and friendly, no longer seemed appropriate. My professional role, once taken for granted, became suddenly inapt.

Life's experiences had not prepared me for the sudden loss of personal congruency. Disorientated and sick from culture shock, I couldn't fathom what ailed me. It made no sense that I could experience such disorientation in the country where I was born and raised.

I yearned for contact with home, my only source of consolation. The store truck yielded its bounty almost every week — a bag of official correspondence for the clinic, mixed with mail for me. Generous family and friends wrote loving cards full of good wishes, and letters in which they described their lives and daily rounds in satisfying detail. There were laboriously pencilled notes from Claire, in Year Two at school, and drawings from Jane, a preschooler. Once, mail from my daughter included a page covered with the alphabet letters of Jane's name, all shakily executed in different colours and sizes. I loved these letters, pressed them to my face, was grateful.

After Jigalong, I would recognise the painful symptoms of culture shock when I travelled with people who were confronted, for the first time, with a culture different from their own. On one holiday in Asia, a friend surprised me when she threw herself on her home-stay bed in tears.

'You don't understand how I feel,' she sobbed. 'I feel so sick. In the street, the minute I step outside the hotel, strangers press in on me. They want me to buy their rubbish or go in their taxis. All I want is to go home.'

She tried but could not change her flight, and rang her son daily. We spent a miserable time together instead of the holiday we'd anticipated so happily. But I did understand.

In my early days at Jigalong, I could imagine no escape. I longed for the old, familiar things. The meagre possessions I'd taken with me, excessive as they might have seemed to others, did little to console me. My longing was a thirst I couldn't slake. The desert to which I'd come with such eagerness was, for a while, an arid region metaphorically as well as literally.

The culture and way of life at Jigalong, with roots deep in the past, were as different from my own as those in any Third World region. Reading about Aboriginal spirituality and culture had not prepared me for the customs and kinship patterns I saw all around me. It was as if what was in my head and my heart no longer matched. Language barriers exacerbated the difficulty. While everyone else spoke three or more languages fluently, English, their last language, was all I knew. We struggled to understand each other. The old Martu people spoke only languages I could not understand at all. In time, I'd begin to recognise a few words, learn a few signals, but I'm still ashamed that the possibility that I could learn seriously to speak Martu Wangka never crossed my mind.

51

There was so much I didn't know, so many things I thought I'd never figure out. And, day and night, there was the inexorable stress of strangers demanding more of my attention than I thought I could possibly provide. The boundaries between my personal life and those of the Martu people seemed to dissolve. Previously, I'd been able to separate my work from my private life, but Martu custom recognised no such distinction. Being available, being willing to share what one had, was part of an intricate social system, and I was caught up in reciprocal relationships, although I didn't know how to engage with the generosity of the Martu people.

Perversely, it amused me that the school, store and office managed to open and close at regular times but, as well as working office hours, the nurse was always on call. The missionaries had run a hospital with beds for several in-patients. When the mission withdrew, the state government employed its own nurses, but the hospital was closed when it became impossible to roster nurses around the clock in such a remote area. Patients who needed hospital care were to be sent or taken to Newman or flown to Port Hedland.

Community nurses were employed as primary carers. These nurses soon acceded to the community's demand for more intensive care, and a de facto twenty-four-hour health service resulted. The system seemed to work reasonably well when there were two nurses at Jigalong to take turns at being on call. It meant each of them had alternate evenings and weekends free. But for a solitary, inexperienced nurse, any time away from the workplace seemed out of the question.

I wrote to my father:

At night, I sleep in a pair of shorts and a T-shirt, ready to open the door quickly. Otherwise, there's a danger it will be broken down.

I lie on my bed and try not to think about the discomfort of culture shock that threatens to choke me. In the end, I think it will be the cultural differences, not clinical difficulties, that will undo me.

To distract myself, I think how hot and dry it is — too dry here for mosquitoes, and I haven't seen a cockroach since Port Hedland. That's no small blessing. I listen to the geckoes barking as they scuttle around inside my room, up and down the walls and in the clothes cupboard. Apparently if you hear a gecko bark seven times you will be blessed with good luck. I count series of barks, but never hear more than four, or at the most five. When I hear five, I wonder if I've lost concentration, perhaps even dozed off.

Sometimes enormous ants cover the verandah floor and I'm afraid to go outside until I've exterminated them with the powerful insect spray I found in a cupboard, left by someone who lived in this flat before I came.

Years later, when I'd moved to the south coast of Western Australia and no longer worked as a nurse, I often woke at night, startled from some dream, imagining I'd heard people banging on my fly-wire door, demanding that I get up and provide assistance. The pattern was set from the first night I was alone.

'This is not an emergency,' I tell the young man standing at my door, asking for a band-aid.

'But it's bleeding,' he says piteously. 'See!' He holds up a finger so I can inspect a small cut.

'You won't bleed to death from that.'

'No,' he agrees cheerfully. 'But I want a band-aid.'

We traipse over to the clinic and I open the door in the dark, go to a cupboard and find an adhesive plaster. I'm afraid, alone with this strange man in the middle of the night. No one else in the settlement is awake and no one is close enough to hear if I shout.

'Don't wake me again for trivial things,' I say as I turn to go back to the flat.

A while later an old man leaning on a walking stick knocks.

'No pills,' he greets me when I stumble to the door.

'What pills?' I ask. I'm groggy from deep sleep and scarcely understand his English.

'Blood pressure. The doctor said I had to take 'em every morning,' he says, waving an empty tablet bottle in the air.

'Did you take the last one yesterday morning?'

'Might be three days ago. Maybe more.'

'So why have you woken me now? It would be better to see me when the clinic's open.'

'I think about it when I wake up in the night.'

Wearily, I open the clinic and sort through a shelf full of prescription medications and find a bottle with his name on it.

Just as the sky begins to lighten, a girl of around fourteen or fifteen wakes me, asking for a tablet for a headache.

'It can wait,' I snap. 'I'm not going to the clinic.'

'Sister . . .' she begins, a plaintive whine starting.

'I don't care. Go away!'

Later in the day, I packed a first-aid box, not for clients, but for myself. In it I put everything I might need in the night. I placed the box by the back door. Although I was woken every night, I could stay home in comfort, going to the clinic only when there were genuine emergencies, not for trivial disturbances. After the first time I was woken for a condom, I added a couple of packets of those to the box, too.

Margaret had been a remote area nurse so long that her skills were honed, routines regular and responses reflexive. In her eagerness to leave, her handover was sketchy. She hadn't seen a need to leave me with more than a page of notes. Or perhaps she told me much more than I absorbed or recorded in my notebook. In any case, I floundered. I couldn't find written policies or procedures describing my responsibilities or how the clinic was run, and no guidelines that might have helped me sort out the bureaucratic aspects of the work, including my responsibility for the work performed by the health workers or the conditions under which they were employed. After several weeks, when I'd consulted with the RFDS about patients whenever I was in doubt, Jane, the community health doctor, pointed out that I should contact her in Newman, not the RFDS, for minor consultations, as we were both employed by the same organisation. She was obviously frustrated by my lack of understanding of the system, and I felt even more confused after our discussion than I had been before.

If I had been less anxious to please the community and the organisation that employed me, I'd have asserted my right to time away from the settlement. If, like the teachers and other non-Aboriginal workers, I'd gone to Newman for an occasional weekend, to socialise and laze by the resort swimming pool and sleep undisturbed as long as I needed, the outcome of my sojourn in Jigalong would have been different.

But then, I thought I'd only be by myself for a few weeks.

9

Somehow I struggled along, working harder than I'd have thought possible. Diagnosing illnesses and prescribing medications in Australia were the prerogative of medical practitioners, and so were ordering X-rays and pathology examinations. Every day, I broke the law and found it stressful.

'I thought only medical practitioners in this state could diagnose and prescribe,' I'd said, naively, to Margaret before she left.

'Well, who will do it if you don't?' she'd answered.

My queries to the doctor in Newman and the authorities in Port Hedland went unanswered; perhaps their silence was itself an admission that there was no adequate answer. And without enough doctors in remote areas of the outback, indeed who else was there but nurses? The compromise, at Jigalong and in other remote settlements, was for nurses to ask visiting doctors to sign off, retrospectively, on decisions made by the nurses in the doctors' absence.

I provided antibiotics for chest and urinary tract infections, skin eruptions and syphilis. I dressed boils, cuts, sores, abrasions and wounds; syringed whole and dismembered flies from the ear canals of babies and small children at the rate of two a day; administered oral fluids to rehydrate infants and old folk who had frequent episodes of diarrhoea or vomiting. I ministered to women who had been beaten by their menfolk. I took blood samples for pathology examinations; applied scabies treatments; filed pathology reports; managed everyone's Medicare cards; deloused heads; bathed babies who were overheated; beat off dogs; ordered and packed away supplies that arrived on the store truck; liaised with hospitals in Newman, Port Hedland and Perth for appointments with consultants, and regularly drove the ambulance to the airstrip. Some of the old folk liked to have their rheumatic joints and aching backs rubbed with liniment, so I did that, too.

Jill-of-all-trades, when the nursing work was finished I did the laundry, cleaned the clinic, and kept the small patch of grass green with water from a primitive reticulation system that I constantly repaired. On the end of the back verandah of the clinic, open to the community, was a bathroom, which housed what were often the only working shower and public toilet in the settlement. I hated cleaning that room, which was always filthy and littered with toilet paper and rubbish. Sometimes the walls, floor and fittings were smeared with faeces. Some days, the plugholes were blocked with soap and the toilet with T-shirts and rags. Once I had to call a plumber to come from Newman to replace the shattered basin and replace taps torn from the wall, leaving water to run unchecked onto the floor.

Highly refined, store-bought food had replaced traditional bush tucker, which was now an occasional treat. People no longer walked the long distances necessary to hunt or gather food. The pastoral station started by the missionaries had been shut down after the community was ordered to shoot all the cattle when the mob had contracted a highly contagious disease that threatened the wellbeing of other stock in the region.

Men once active as jackaroos and overseers at Jigalong and on other pastoral stations no longer worked. A so-called 'thrifty gene' enabled hunters and gatherers to use their limited and intermittent nutrition effectively, and to retain excess calories as a survival mechanism for the times when food was not available. Now it worked with their high-fat, high-carbohydrate diet so that obesity, diabetes, hypertension and heart disease were endemic. White settlers had introduced infectious diseases previously not experienced by Aboriginal people. Life expectancy was, at best, fifteen to twenty years less than that of other Australians.

The clinic's clients considered their health to be my business, not their responsibility. If I gave them medication or suggested ways they could improve their diet or increase their exercise, they shuffled and looked uncomfortable, as if they thought I shirked my responsibility. I wondered if perhaps they were unconsciously employing a form of resistance to yet more whitefella interventions in lives severely affected by colonisation. It's unlikely they'd have been able to articulate their reluctance to comply with my bossy directives.

I quickly learned not to expect my clients to take prescribed medication consistently, nor to modify lifestyle choices that would make their diseases worse. Everyone continued their sedentary lives and consistently ate refined food full of fat and sugar. Sometimes people with diabetes gave themselves prescribed insulin, often they did not. People with respiratory disease smoked cigarettes. Parents did not administer medications regularly, if at all, to children with chest infections or diarrhoea. Their choices often provoked the doctor into irritation with me. She seemed, like them, to regard the compliance of her patients as my responsibility.

I tried gluing diagrams representing sunrise, midday and sunset on packets of tablets and bottles of medicine, to remind people to take their medication at those times. They looked interested. But they returned to the clinic, their condition deteriorated, with full packets of tablets, and bottles of mixture untouched, often lost. They expected me to do what needed to be done to cure them, with my Western-style health care, while they remained passive.

Years later, writing this, I recognise the futility of much that was done in the hope of improving the health of the people of Jigalong. I provided first aid, and several times that immediate care helped to save a life. At first I thought I had some of the answers to endemic poor health, but my optimism only showed I didn't understand the depth of the problems, not only in health, but in all aspects of the lives of the people whose rich culture had inevitably been altered through colonisation. For my clients, personal health could not be separated from the health of their land and their relationship to it.

I felt wedged between conflicting standards. The Health Department and the community itself demanded from me a form of patriarchal behaviour that was diametrically opposed to my personal philosophy of nursing, a strongly held belief that the role of a nurse is to work with people whose responsibility it is to look after themselves to whatever extent they are able.

Appropriately, parents advocated for their children and younger women for old people, especially when the old men and women spoke no English. But I was amused when young men and young women came in pairs to the clinic, and the healthy person acted as spokesperson for the one who was ill. Perhaps there was a taboo about discussing their own personal health or illness, or maybe it was simply considered bad form.

'She's got a problem,' an advocate says, pointing with her chin to her friend.

The other woman stands, submissive, picking the skin around her fingernails.

'What sort of problem?'

'Sick every day. Can't eat.'

'How many days since she ate properly?'

'Coupla weeks, maybe.'

I wonder if she's pregnant, but don't know how to ask. I haven't been here long enough to know what's appropriate, even when I'm being consulted. Perhaps pregnancy is a taboo subject.

'Baby?' I ask. No answer.

'Does she still bleed?'

The spokesperson shakes her head.

Only the deaths of very old people or young babies were ascribed to natural causes. If an individual died accidentally or as the result of unexpected illness, blame was apportioned. Parents whose children died in hospital, or because they had not been taken to hospital, drivers of vehicles that crashed, relatives of those who suicided or killed themselves accidentally were all held responsible and punished or paid back, often severely. Even the nurses in remote areas could be held responsible for unforeseen deaths.

Many other deaths were attributed to sorcery inflicted by malevolent spirits known as 'feather feet' because of the moccasins they wore to cover their tracks. To counteract the evil performed by spirits, *mabarn* men — who possessed healing and other magical powers — visited the sick in order to cure them. I sensed the community would have preferred me to perform similar magical cures. Sometimes, working with a patient who was seriously ill or badly injured, I would recognise as a *mabarn* one of the mature men sitting quietly in the treatment room.

They regarded me with grave benevolence. As a white woman, I could not be privy to the ways they performed their healing ministration. That occurred secretly, perhaps when I was out of the room. The *mabarn* men did not interfere with my white nurse work; patients who were conscious gained confidence and comfort from them, and so, in some inexplicable way, did I.

★　　★　　★

PW and Joannie were kind and generous, although they must also have been curious about a nurse with so little experience who relied so heavily on them for simple instructions. If they felt burdened by my nervousness and lack of expertise, they didn't show it. Instead, they steered me gently and with abundant good humour in the direction they thought I should go, suggesting and modelling the behaviour they wanted from me. They took it in turns to prompt and cajole me to work under their expert tutelage. They were amazingly tolerant, given my obvious lack of proficiency and my dazed condition.

Every weekday morning, unless customary law matters or personal business meant they were out of the settlement or not available, one or the other appeared ready for work. PW showered in the bathroom at the clinic and arrived smelling of soap, with water dripping from his hair. In the absence of a towel on which to dry himself, his clean jeans and T-shirt were always damp. Joannie frequently brought a child or two with her, and they played around the clinic while she worked.

I've forgotten about the doctor's clinic until she pulls up in the driveway.

'Hello,' I say, feeling apprehensive.

'G'day. What a terrible drive! The road's cut up even worse than last time,' she complains.

'I haven't done anything special to prepare for your clinic,' I confess.

'Margaret would have left you instructions about it.'

'She may well have done, but I haven't found them.'

'I suppose we'll have to do the best we can, then,' she snaps as she opens the back door of her car and drags out her bag. 'Are the health workers here?'

'I haven't seen them, but I'm sure they won't be far away.'

'Mmm. I like your optimism. Anyway, let's get started.'

Jane doesn't suffer fools gladly, I think, following her across to the clinic and opening the door. She's touchy this morning. I hope it won't be too bad, in spite of my lack of preparation.

I pull out a file marked DOCTOR'S CLINIC, and open it to a list of names under the previous week's date. Some of the names have asterisks beside them, and the words 'Follow up' scribbled in the margins. At least I have a place to start, but no idea how I'll find anyone, unless they come voluntarily. In another file, marked RESEARCH, I find another list. This is a record of people who will have their weight and blood pressure measured (by me) before the doctor examines them. It's a once-a-month event, as part of an ongoing survey set up from Perth, or perhaps from Port Hedland. I'm sure the scientists are well meaning and their research important. But some of the Martu people are bewildered by all the attention which seems to have little personal relevance for them, and others find it irksome and intrusive.

There's something odd about both lists, and it takes a couple of seconds before I work it out. The word *Nyabaru* occurs in about one in three names. It seems to be a first or last name, but occasionally it's in both columns, so there must be a number of men and women whose name is *Nyabaru Nyabaru*. Many of the younger children have names similar to those of children of their ages in the wider community but, almost without exception, the children's names sound wrong when I say them out loud, distorted somehow. The spelling is weird.

I don't have time to worry too much about the clinic, because Joannie arrives in time to save me from the feared wrath of the doctor. She quickly organises the rooms and tells me what to expect and what to do. Both are apparently to Jane's liking, because she doesn't complain. Meanwhile, PW arrives and

Joannie sends him in the Nissan to collect people to be followed up from the last visit. Soon, an informal queue of men, women and children overflows onto the verandah and down the path.

'Can't you hurry?' Jane asks.

'Sorry,' I mumble. I feel like a junior nurse rebuked by the ward sister.

'You'll have to do better than this,' she scolds.

The morning drags on and I muddle my way into the early afternoon. By then I'm exhausted. I'm relieved when Jane refuses my offer of lunch.

'How can so many people be called *Nyabaru*?' I ask PW and Joannie after she leaves. 'Is it a special Martu name?'

'That's the name we use when a person's passed away. Can't use their proper name then,' PW says, with a rocking movement of his hand, held palm down at waist height, that I'll come to recognise as meaning 'someone has died', even when the words are not said.

'Not even for someone still alive, who has that name?'

'That's right. Can't use it anymore.'

'Is that why the children have names that are spelled and sound different from other names I know? So they won't have to be *Nyabaru*?'

'Yo. And that's why he can't use his name,' Joannie says, pointing her chin in PW's direction. 'Two mens with his names passed away. Now he just has initials.'

'Yo,' PW adds. 'Should be *Nyabaru Nyabaru*, too. But the Health Department says I must have proper names. For the records. That's in clinic.'

'Is that all right with you?' I inquire.

He looks at his feet, raises one shoulder a centimetre or two. 'Yo,' he says after a moment.

10

One of the first things PW taught me was to take blood samples, bush style. All specimens had to be transported to the pathologist at the hospital in Newman, and anyone who looked like a reliable courier was recruited for the task. The community coordinator and the staff from the store, whose work took them to the town regularly, were obvious choices; but visiting police officers, social workers, builders and tradespeople were all persuaded, on different occasions, to deliver blood and other specimens kept cool in transit with an ice pack in a blue polystyrene lunch box.

'Today, we get blood,' PW announces one morning.

'Tell me about that,' I ask, puzzled. I don't remember being told I had to collect blood samples.

'Need to check if the antibiotics worked. Them young fellas got syphilis,' he explains.

'Do the young men come to the clinic?'

'Nah. We go to them.'

'What happens to the clinic?'

'I tol' Joannie. She'll come by'n'by.'

PW's method for obtaining blood samples (and, I'll discover later, for other procedures) is unorthodox and efficient. When he's filled an esky with ice packs from the freezer and added bundles of sterile syringes, test tubes and alcohol wipes, we climb into the Nissan Patrol.

The vehicle isn't old, but it's full of dust that clings to everything, and smells of unwashed bodies. It rattles, even though we drive at walking pace. This is my first official foray into the settlement, and I'm grateful PW is driving. He's taken charge of the venture and I feel safe. It feels good to have a clear purpose, rather than so many amorphous responsibilities that I don't quite comprehend.

Away from the clinic, past the school and the store, I'm aware of packs of mangy-looking dogs with patches of hair missing. Flies encrust the sores on their backs and ears. The animals bark menacingly and snap at the tyres as we drive past. These are the only domesticated animals in the place, and there can't be a family here that doesn't have a dog or two.

'Them dogs nearly all got shot a while ago, eh,' PW remarks. 'But we said No, and whitefellas came from Port Hedland with Aboriginal environmental health workers. Now the dogs won't get fleas and worms, so kids don't get them, eh. Might look better, too, by'n'by,' he laughs.

We pass buildings with a disconcerting air of impermanence, although there have been people living here for almost a century. There are a few larger buildings, in poor condition because of graffiti and other acts of vandalism that have smashed doors and windows and punctured walls. There are groups of shacks constructed of rusty iron and with no windows, huts without doors, and an occasional bush shelter. Local government building codes do not apply in Jigalong, and there is no systematic repair program.

'People camp close to their own country, when they can,' PW informs me. 'Ever since the mission first came, a long time ago, eh. Now we are all the same. The Jigalong mob.'

He doesn't tell me that Jigalong, with its Martu population, is actually in Palyku country, to the west of Martu country. Nor does he tell me that it's less than thirty years since a group of seventeen women and children, who had lived nomadic lives far from contact with white people, were brought to Jigalong from Martu country in the Western Desert.

Grubby mattresses and pillows are stacked untidily on verandahs, away from the dogs. Before dark the bedding will be spread again on the ground outside, where family groups gather every night until the weather turns wet or too cold. Then they'll move inside, to sleep crowded together on the floor. Campfires, the closest thing most families have to a kitchen, are built near the dwellings. This morning, some still smoke. One has a billy attached to a tripod over it; the water boils robustly, spills over and hisses as it hits the hot coals. There's a tiny patch of grass outside one hut, incongruous in the red dirt. As we drive closer, I see it has been carefully cut.

At the far end of the settlement, there's a small group of conventional prefabricated houses and here, too, bedding is piled on the verandahs. The houses are surrounded by wire fences, separating neighbours in a way counter to the traditional custom of Martu sharing. Someone has thrown a few faded T-shirts and some jeans carelessly over a fence to dry and stiffen in the sun. I'm dying to ask PW where he lives and who lives in the new houses, but I'm mindful of my manners and my propensity to pry. He volunteers no information. I remind myself to close my mouth when I become aware that I'm gaping. After I've been here longer, I'll find that an emerging class system at Jigalong dictates who lives in what part of the settlement.

Six or seven adults sit facing each other on two mattresses under a tree. They ignore the toddlers rolling in the dust. The men and women are holding hands of cards.

'They're playin' poker,' PW informs me. 'It's pension day.'

Dodging dogs and children, he pulls up outside a hut and points with his chin towards a young man who's watching us from where he leans lethargically against a wall.

'I need some blood,' I say.

There's no point in beating about the bush. We have ten more patients to find and it's almost time for PW to go home for the day. The young man pulls up his sleeve without saying a word. He braces himself against the wall and I clean the area over a vein that I hope will be easy to bleed. It takes six pre-packed alcohol wipes before I'm satisfied I've scrubbed away enough desert dust and sweat. PW hands me a rubber tourniquet and I apply it above the fellow's elbow. I pull on sterile gloves from a packet PW tears open when he sees I'm ready. The man stares implacably over my shoulder while I insert the needle and undo the rubber band. It's the first time I've done this, but I'm not telling anyone. I'm surprised when the blood flows freely. I quickly transfer it to the test tube, invert it several times to mix blood and chemicals and hand the tube to PW, who applies a sticky identity label and puts it in the esky.

'That wasn't too bad, was it?' I ask.

The young man inclines his head slightly. He clearly doesn't want to engage in conversation. I persist; after all I'm new at this. I'm a conscientious community health nurse and client education is a high priority. I provide a short, unwelcome information session.

'This illness is highly contagious,' I say. 'That means it's easy to pass from one person to another.'

He continues to ignore me.

'Use condoms,' I admonish. 'Every time.'

I jump out of the ridiculously high vehicle nine more times, and bleed people on their own doorsteps (or whatever is the equivalent for a hut or shack or old car-body-turned-home). In the city, specialist phlebotomists take blood samples, yet here am I, nonchalantly finding veins in clients with dust swirling around us and the sun beating down. If my hospital colleagues could see me now, I think, they'd be impressed. I'm elated: I've managed to accomplish this one thing.

'You're good at this,' I tell PW. 'Thank you. You know everyone, and know exactly where they'll be when we want them.'

'They're my people, eh,' he says simply.

These young men and others returned, ashamed, to the clinic within weeks of every course of penicillin. They invariably complained of a discharge; PW took specimens for culture in the laboratory; and I gave them deep, painful injections. We tried to find a way to prevent reinfection. They'd be even more ashamed when I asked them for the names of contacts who might have passed syphilis on to them. Every time, the men provided only the name of one woman. They told me she did not live in Jigalong, but 'somewhere else'. Not for a minute did I believe only one woman was involved.

When a baby — a two-year-old girl — was brought to the clinic, and her mother told me she had a discharge from her vagina, I worried. Pathology tests showed the child was infected with gonorrhoea. The only way she could have contracted the disease was through sexual assault, and I contacted the health, police and welfare departments. In a phone call from Newman, Jane told me how to treat the child's symptoms with antibiotics.

In a settlement with no resident police or welfare workers, it was impossible to access immediate help, but I expected a rapid response, especially since the victim was only a baby. The police and social workers, no doubt hindered by the unwieldy systems within which they worked, did not come. I demanded and pleaded that someone should deal with this crime because all I could do was treat the child for the disease. I could not find the perpetrator nor stop the abuse. In the end, I was left feeling unsupported, angry, powerless and scared.

II

As though these incidents, culture shock, the intensity of the workload and sleep deprivation weren't enough, I also had to cope with living alone on the edge of the desert. I was shocked to realise that I was the lone outsider and that everyone in the settlement except me had a relationship with others.

Each Martu person belonged to his or her kinship system, and even the smallest children knew where they fitted in the elaborate intergenerational network. The teachers had their colleagues and the principal, who was solicitous of his young charges. The office staff and mechanics had each other to talk to, eat meals with and share the concerns of their day.

Outside the Aboriginal community, I had no idea how to socialise with the other non-Indigenous workers. The few times I'd been away from home, I'd been on holiday with friends or family. With consternation I discovered I had no idea how to form new friendships, especially in what seemed to me to be such a bizarre situation. This was another major problem, but in the end, one solved for me, rather than by me.

The sun is setting, and I'm standing at the kitchen sink, slicing carrots and celery to stir fry for my evening meal. I would have liked to listen to the news, but the single radio station is community controlled and broadcasts nothing but popular music. There's a knock on my door. It's a gentle sound, not the usual deafening din. Wiping my hands wearily, I go to see who is there, prepared to be interrupted again.

'G'day! Hope this isn't too inconvenient,' says the woman standing on the doorstep. Her smile, like her voice, is warm. Middle-aged, she's dressed in freshly pressed turquoise pedal pushers and a matching shirt that complement her reddish hair and fair, freckled skin. 'I'm Sandy. I work in the community office, but I've been in Perth for a break. Got back this afternoon and thought I'd come over and say hello.'

I have to restrain myself from throwing my arms around her; I'm so pleased to see someone who isn't demanding something. But I calmly invite her in and put the kettle on in an automatic action. She settles herself comfortably, her elbows on the table, and I feel as if we've been friends for a long time. Before the water has boiled, I've begun to tell her about the past week and how hard it has been.

'It's a pity you nurses have to be so available,' she says sympathetically. 'We keep proper business hours in the office. If some real catastrophe happens, or if you guys need the strip lit up so the plane can land, we'll be there. But it has to be pretty damned major to get any of us out after hours.'

'I don't know how Margaret kept going,' I say. 'No wonder she needed a holiday.'

'It's her life. She's been here for years and lives and breathes the work. But I've seen other nurses, much younger than you, if you don't mind me saying, burn out really quickly.'

Sandy tells me she's been at Jigalong for almost a year and that she manages the Community Development and Employment Program, which pays funds to community members through the Aboriginal and Torres Strait Islander Commission.

'Is that like the parenting payment?'

'No, people get that too. CDEP was developed to benefit remote communities where there's not enough real employment, but it's not only available in remote areas. It's meant to create employment opportunities and teach whitefella skills to Aboriginal people. The major focus is "to maintain, preserve or restore the cultural integrity of the community" — something like that, anyway. People do up to twenty hours' community work a week and get paid for it.'

'What a great scheme,' I enthuse.

'Well, it would be. But no one has to account for what they do, so there's not really much point in anyone actually doing anything. They get enough money through other government funding, like the unemployment and parenting payments, anyway.'

I pour more coffee. In the distance, some children call to each other.

'Traditional cultural activities are classed as "work" under the CDEP, so people can claim it if they are planning ceremonies or shooting kangaroos. Everyone around here calls it "sit-down money" because they don't really have to *do* anything. Although I work for the Council, I've come to see it's throwing money at a problem, not solving it. Almost everyone here is dependent on welfare, in one way or another.'

By the time Sandy left an hour later, I could see my chances of survival were less shaky. I'd enjoyed talking to her and finding out about the community. Not only that, her information gave me the idea of employing people to clean the clinic and water the garden, paying them with CDEP funds. That would free me to do more health education and preventative work. After much negotiation with Sandy, two women came for a day or two, but then told me they weren't keen to work in the clinic. In the end, I decided it was easier to factor the time into my day and do the extra tasks myself than it was to rely on people who preferred not to do the sort of menial work I offered. They knew they'd get paid, anyway.

I returned Sandy's visit a few days later. Her caravan had been plonked in the centre of a large vacant block between two houses. Sally and Ian lived on one side and Ray, the community coordinator, on the other. The way from the clinic to the caravan was across the wide main 'street' and down an alleyway between three-metre-high wire-mesh fences. On my first visit I was startled to see the femur of a very large beast beside the path, partly hidden under a burden of rubbish. There was no odour, not even from the carelessly discarded dirty nappies and other trash, because the atmosphere was so dry and the heat so intense that everything left exposed dried within an hour or two, leaving nothing for odour-forming bacteria to live on.

'It might have been from a steer,' Ray said when I asked him later. 'Though who knows how it got there.'

'I was shocked when I first arrived,' Sandy tells me over the chicken salad she's prepared. 'My department said there'd be accommodation. I have to pay, of course, but I thought I'd have somewhere comfortable to live. Imagine how I felt when I found I'd be living in a caravan!'

'My flat's luxury, after this,' I say, looking around. 'But you've made the caravan very comfortable with all your lovely things. You've even managed to soften the brown of the furnishings.'

'The brown!' we say together, and laugh.

'I've lived in all sorts of places,' Sandy says. 'My husband was a lighthouse keeper, and we had some interesting experiences. Once, when our children were little, I even spent a couple of years on tiny islands off the east coast of Australia. The ships that brought the supplies only came once a month in good weather, and not at all through winter. Now, that's isolation, I can tell you.' She laughs again, an infectious chuckle.

'You sound like a real adventurer.'

'Yes. They were good days, but it was harrowing when the kids were sick. But if you plan to stay, you have to make yourself a home wherever you are, or you don't survive long.'

'You've done it very well. Do you spend much time outside under the awnings?'

'No, not really. I insisted on having them when I first got here. It took months before they arrived. And then I found that every time I sat outside, the locals would see it as an invitation to come and visit. And I don't like to encourage uninvited guests.' She passes me the salad bowl, and then helps herself.

'Sometimes, I get a bit scared, really,' she resumes. 'I'm a long way from everyone else and the caravan is pretty damned flimsy. Anyone who wanted to could break in easily. But so far I've been all right. And the coordinator looks out for me from his house.'

'I've survived two weeks by myself,' I boast after we've cleared the table and folded it to make a settee at one end of the van.

I'd dealt with everyone who'd presented at the clinic. The day before, I'd helped to run the doctor's clinic. There'd been no serious injuries or illnesses. Most days, my lunch hour had been uninterrupted, and I'd kept the clinic reasonably clean. The health workers had come to work on the days they were supposed to. My confidence had increased.

'I'm looking forward to the weekend, although I'm certain to be disturbed,' I tell Sandy.

'You could always open the clinic for an hour or two. If you get the health workers to tell people, they might come in the morning and not straggle in all day.'

'That's a good idea. Thanks. It's worth a try.'

12

My first patient on Saturday morning is a woman I guess is in her early thirties, but it's hard to tell. Her hair is dishevelled and dull with dust. Her faded khaki T-shirt is covered in dried blood and dirt. She looks ill and she's hot to my touch.

'My arm's sore,' she says. She's cupping her right elbow with her left hand. 'And my head, too. It aches.' I help her to a chair, and she sits heavily and rearranges herself gingerly, until she's leaning forward with her arm resting in her lap. I can see she's in a lot of pain.

'Point to where your head hurts,' I instruct.

She touches the top of her head where her curls are tangled and matted with dried blood.

'Let me see,' I say, moving closer. She raises her hand to protect herself. 'I'll be gentle,' I promise. 'But I must see what I'm doing before I can fix it.'

I collect a pair of sharp scissors, a bowl of warm saline and some gauze, and put them on a tray. It can't be too bad, I reassure myself as I prepare the equipment, or she wouldn't have been able to walk in here. Putting the tray beside the woman, I pull on a pair of sterile gloves to protect myself as much as her while I clean the wound. She cowers away from me. I coax her to take deep breaths and sit still while I work. It's twenty minutes before I've cleaned and cut away enough of her hair so that I can see what's underneath. I'm appalled at the extent of the wound.

'This is very nasty,' I say, but I'm thinking, My God, she's been battered. 'How did this happen?' I ask, trying to sound non-committal. She hangs her head, and doesn't answer.

'What caused this bad sore on your head?' I ask again.

'He flogged me,' she whispers at last, and her head droops lower. I can see she's ashamed because someone has battered her. As if it is *her* fault.

'That's dreadful. No one deserves to be flogged. Who hit you?'

'My *nuba*,' she whispers.

'Your husband?'

'Yo.'

My stomach clenches and I feel a wave of nausea, but know I must control it. I can't be sick now, however scared and angry and impotent I feel. I might fear and loathe men who assault women, but right now I have a job to do. There'll be time later to feel angry.

'How did you get to the clinic?'

'He brought me. In a car.'

I'm curious about the man who'd violently assaulted this woman, then driven her to the clinic. I'm confident he won't hurt me. Most likely, by the time he'd brought her to Jigalong from an outstation hundreds of kilometres from here, he'd have been full of remorse and promises. Those who have not experienced family violence will not understand, but those who have will know that he would have pleaded with her. Like many men who bash their partners, he'd have begged her to forgive him, told her he was very sorry, and that he hadn't meant to hurt her. He'd have promised her it would never happen again. He'd believe what he'd said, and so would she. He'd have urged her to get attention at the clinic, then driven her in his car to the front gate, so she wouldn't have to walk from wherever he'd decided they should camp in the settlement.

When she goes back to him after her injuries have been attended to, he'll be solicitous and they'll be happy together for a time. But then the tension will build and she'll provoke him until he lashes out and hurts her again.

'Hold still,' I tell her. 'I'll be as gentle as I can. I'll try not to hurt you.'

I need to gauge the extent of her wound. Cautiously, I put my left hand on the top of her skull and feel the pulpy tissue realign itself. Gently I pull on a tuft of hair with my right hand. A flap lifts right away, exposing an ugly secret. There's a wide wound that covers the top of her skull. It takes a while to register what I'm looking at. Where I'd expected to see a necrotic mess, the flesh under the flap is surprisingly clean. But deep inside, there is movement. I look closer, and see fat cream-coloured maggots wriggling.

An entomologist would have known exactly how long they'd been there. But I can only guess from their size that the wound was flyblown at least twenty-four hours before. When the weather is warm, blowflies are attracted to unprotected wounds and other moist areas, where they lay their eggs. Blowflies at Jigalong laid eggs in the pus and debris in infected ears of the children, as well as in wounds. Before I left, I learned to deal with them with equanimity, cleaning wounds and syringing ears to flush out maggots and dismembered fragments of flies that had driven the children to poke in their ears with sticks and pencils in futile attempts to rid themselves of the maddening insects.

The maggots have done a good job in the woman's wound. They've secreted enzymes to liquefy the necrotic flesh and disinfected it with a bacteria-killing protein, before they consumed the damaged flesh. They are not sterile, of course, but if it hadn't been for them, by now the wound would have been gangrenous and putrid.

She must hear the sharp intake of my breath, but I don't tell her about the infestation. She's been traumatised enough already and doesn't need the disturbing information. I don't know how to remove the maggots without causing more damage, so I let the flap of flesh drop back. It almost conceals the wound, and I cover the top of her head with a large combine dressing bandaged in place. It probably won't do any good, but the activity makes me feel better.

'There,' I say. 'That's done.' She'll need a general anaesthetic before a surgeon will be able to clean her wound, but that's many hours away. 'I'll give you some painkillers and make you a cup of tea.'

She smiles weakly and leans back.

'Why didn't you come before?' I ask as she drinks the sweet milky tea from the mug she holds with both hands. She's very thirsty, and I wonder how long she's been without food and drink. Could be days, by the look of her.

'We were camped out. Very far. My *nuba*. Him not want to come.'

'It's good you're here now, anyway.' I sit down where she can see me without moving her head. 'Tell me what happened.'

'Him very angry. Drink wine. From flagon. Then he hit me.'

'What with?' I coach.

'Star picket.'

'He's sliced the top of your head. It's bad. I've patched you up for now, but I can't fix it. We'll get the Flying Doctor to take you to hospital.'

She nods and whispers, 'OK.'

Before I ring the RFDS base, almost as an afterthought, I check the rest of her body. After the first time, she hasn't complained of pain, except for her head, but I discover she has a broken humerus as well as multiple bruises and abrasions. I splint her right arm between shoulder and elbow to stabilise the broken bone. She says it feels more comfortable.

The plane arrives within an hour, diverted on its way to Port Hedland from collecting a stockman injured in an accident on one of the stations further north. While we wait, I do what I can to treat the lacerations and bruises on the woman's arms and legs and back.

Flogging was not a word I'd often come across before Jigalong, except in the vernacular, as in 'to flog a dead horse'. I thought it was an unusual word for my patient to use. I associated it with penal settlements, convicts and history. But I would discover that Aboriginal people associated it with the discipline meted out earlier this century by overzealous missionaries. Children, who were supposed to be in the care of these white people, were flogged for misdemeanours as minor as speaking in their own languages when they'd been told not to. At Jigalong, 'floggen', used as a noun, was a word in common currency.

Flogging and spearing were sanctioned by the Martu people as just punishment for transgressions against the Law. Physical punishment was a form of restorative justice, designed to repair wrongs and restore the health and strength of the community. Punishment endorsed by the community was administered under the supervision of the elders, who monitored the severity. But physical violence, sometimes severe and often inflicted by people under the influence of alcohol, was also used to settle arguments or in an attempt to control others. Women came to the clinic for treatment following altercations in which they'd been beaten up by irate men, who sometimes claimed authority to administer punishment under customary law, even though the Law did not allow such abuse.

A week after she'd gone to Port Hedland, the woman returned to Jigalong, still moving cautiously. Her scalp had been cleaned and sutured and her broken bones set in the operating theatre at the regional hospital. I was appalled when I read in the hospital's discharge letter that she'd also sustained a fractured left elbow. In my consternation at the severity of the attack, and in the face of her stoic acceptance of pain, I'd completely missed the second fracture.

Like most other victims of family violence in the settlement, she declined to go to the police to make a complaint, although in Port Hedland she would have been supported by one of the hospital social workers. As I suspected, her husband had made extravagant promises about never harming her again. In any case, she had kinship responsibilities towards him, and going to the police would cause her shame. And, even if she'd wanted to leave, there was nowhere she could go to be safe after she complained. Anyway, she doubted, probably with justification, that her complaint would be taken seriously.

13

Within hours, there's another challenge.

'Sick baby, Sis,' an old woman says as she thrusts a dirty, inert bundle towards me. There's a young woman, hardly past puberty, at the old woman's side. She's mumbling something I don't understand.

'Let me see,' I say. I'm surprised at the firm tone of my voice. 'Let me look at this little baby.'

'Bin sick for two days now in bush,' the old woman volunteers.

'Does she have a name yet?' I ask, as if it matters.

The woman shrugs. She says nothing.

I take the child from her outstretched arms, willing myself to act confidently. I feel a sharp buzz of adrenaline; it starts behind my eyes. This is the terrible moment I've been anticipating, the emergency I won't be able to manage. Blood pounds in my head. The woman and I look at each other over the tiny form in my arms and I don't bother to try to reassure her. She won't believe me. We both know how sick the baby is. We know she's close to death. Across cultures, we share the fear and the wisdom of old women.

I'm afraid the baby will die in the clinic. I calculate quickly: it will after nightfall before the RFDS arrives on the airstrip, at least another hour before they'll take off again. Fear, octopus-like, seizes and squashes me. It crushes the breath from my chest and paralyses me.

I could be charged with negligence if the baby dies. I'll be hauled in front of the Coroner's Court and my incompetence exposed to the world. I'm an impostor, a registered nurse with too little experience in dealing with accidents and emergencies and no training in paediatric nursing. And I've put myself in a position of responsibility. The Coroner will find the baby died by my hand and I'll be charged with manslaughter. Or worse.

The Nurses' Registration Board will have no option but to strike me from their register. My shame will be spread across the newspapers for everyone to read. If there's any benefit, there'll be changes to the practice of appointing nurses to remote area posts. Perhaps they'll develop policies and procedures for recruiting only highly skilled nurse practitioners, the type of professionals that the people in communities remote from hospitals and doctors deserve. Perhaps nurses will no longer work alone.

This is one of my worst nightmares, the thoughts babble on. If the baby dies before the doctor can get here, her family will accuse me of killing her. There have been stories in professional journals and the general media about nurses who've been chased out of other communities, driving wildly for their lives in departmental vehicles ahead of violent mobs of enraged relatives, for less than the death of a baby. There are rumours about relatives of patients posing serious threats to health care workers.

Automatically, I feel for a pulse in the child's temple, but she's too dehydrated for me to locate one. The skin is taut across her forehead and her fontanelles are sunken. I put my hand on her chest where the stretched neck of her singlet has fallen away, exposing one tiny pink nipple on black skin. I count. Ninety-nine, a hundred, a hundred and one. No, that's wrong! What am I counting? The heartbeat? No, I can't even feel her heart. Her breathing? Dear God! I think. No baby can breathe so fast.

Her eyelids flutter momentarily in her grey face and with a shock I recognise the rhythm of my own crazy pulse, hammering away in my head, chest, fingertips. Her weight flops in my hands, a little baby so recently delivered from the body of her mother, herself little more than a child. Sweat prickles my skin. I feel myself beginning to gag. I swallow. Twice. Take a breath. Steady myself.

'Help me,' I say to the old woman, who's been watching impassively.

She moves closer and we unwrap the bunny rug, once pink but now smeared with dust, grime from many sweaty hands, leaked milk and crusted faeces. With shaking hands, I take off the woollen cardigan, the filthy singlet, a nappy pinned in a haphazard triangle. The nappy is dry and I note a urine stain, yellow and dried. The limp girl-body that should still be in foetal position flattens out. One hand falls on the desk, pink-palmed, fragile. Her ribs are sucked in as she lies fighting for the dust-laden air. Her black eyes are open, sunken and sightless. I reach for the smallest face mask I can find and attach it to an oxygen cylinder. I place the mask over the baby's face and turn the oxygen on, gently, very gently.

She's cold. I've felt other bodies cold like this. But they were worn out bodies, old, sagging, wrinkled. They bided their time in beds in high-rise hospitals until it was time for their owners to give them up.

'Her extremities are cold,' we'd tell each other at shift handovers. 'And her nose,' we might add, nodding sagely as we predicted imminent death.

Those hospitals had high beds, white sheets, pillows, oxygen piped through taps on the walls, and shiny equipment. There were always other people, expert nurses and doctors one could trust, people who'd take or share responsibility. Within easy reach in every corridor, crash carts stood laden with all the equipment anyone could need to deal with an emergency. Three times a day, senior nurses checked the carts, softly reciting the names of pieces of equipment, drugs and dressings, ensuring all was in readiness for an emergency. There were phones, call-bells, and the sure knowledge that, if you signalled, someone would hear and be at your side to help.

There's a phone in the clinic office, but professional help is hundreds of kilometres away and specialist opinion even further.

The baby's mother probably won't care if she dies: she's fourteen, intellectually handicapped; and already she thinks I've given the baby too much attention.

'My eye is sore,' she tells me for the first of what seems like forty times that afternoon.

'I'll look at it later,' I promise.

'Fix it,' she demands. 'Now!'

Her grandmother won't care if the baby dies — she's on the reserve on the edge of Newman, probably lying in a patch of scarce shade beside a shed on an old mattress, a bottle of wine in her hand. The father? He is in Geraldton, where he was born. He's the wrong skin (relationship classification) and he does not have the right to call the mother of his child by the term 'spouse'; their union was wrong. If he thought about it at all, he'd say the baby has no spirit.

She is going to die. I see this reflected in the eyes of the old woman, the great-aunt who's taken responsibility for the family, the young mother and her baby. She's brought them into the settlement on the back of a beaten-up utility from a desert camp, an outstation in the Robertson Range, sixty kilometres away.

'She tol' me it's a silly baby,' the old woman says, pointing with her chin to the girl, who is sitting unconcerned in the next room. 'It won' suck. So she stopped feeding 'im yesterday.'

The baby had a mild chest infection when they brought her to the clinic three days before, but that's developed into something far more sinister, a life-threatening illness, probably pneumonia. It is my fault, because I told the mother and a group of her friends to bring the baby back if she was any worse the next day, naively expecting them to do as I suggested.

I tick off a mental checklist: I can't locate a pulse, and her respirations are irregular and almost imperceptible. The peripheral blood vessel system has shut down. She is dehydrated and can no longer suck. Even if I were confident of my skills, it would be impossible to insert an intravenous infusion because her veins have probably collapsed. It is far too dangerous to insert a gastric tube; she has no swallowing reflex. There is no sign of gastroenteritis, that's something in our favour. Her temperature is very low.

I pull up my shirt and press her cold naked body against my warm sweaty skin. With one hand, I wrap us both in a blanket. The well-washed grey wool scratches my skin and I feel my body heat rise. I don't let myself think what might be on the blanket, or in it, since it was last laundered. I try not to think of the judgement of colleagues if they could see me, as I try to warm this dying baby, as efficiently as I know how, in this forsaken outpost of the health system.

So much for the Nurses' Board and its standards, I think. They do not take into account the conditions in a real-life situation like this.

As I move towards the phone in the next room, the body shudders against my skin. And stops. I sense she's no longer breathing — that she won't breathe again. I snatch away the blanket, take a deep, steadying breath to gather myself, lay the still body back on the bench, extend her tiny neck slightly to let the air into her lungs, and put my face to hers. For several minutes, I breathe into her. Her little chest moves slowly up and down, responsive to the air from my lungs. One-and-two-and-one-and ... I count. Gently, carefully. Puff. Stop. Puff. Stop.

She shudders again, jerks slightly. I move my head sideways and watch her abdomen, willing it to rise by itself. The chest quivers.

She flickers her eyelids, screws up her face to cry, thinks better of it, and lives. Cradled in my arms, she reminds me of a doll I loved as a child. It had a hard china head that drooped backwards away from a body made of cloth, grey from constant contact with my grubby hands. For a time, I preferred her without clothes, and the fabric of her body began to fray. I was mortified when I poked at a small hole and discovered she was stuffed with kapok, like a pillow.

News of the sick baby in the clinic has spread in the settlement and a crowd gathers, clutching cans of Coke and packets of potato crisps. This is the day's entertainment, excitement to liven the hot, boring time between midday and night. Women and children fill the waiting room, edging into the office to watch me as I work. Their faces are solemn and there's a low murmur as they speculate about what's happening. A toddler drops a biscuit in the dirt on the floor and bellows. In the corner, another toddler pulls at his mother's dress. She unbuttons it and he grabs her sagging breast in both hands, directs the nipple into his mouth and sucks greedily.

'My eye's sore,' the baby's mother wails again, resenting the fuss we are making about her daughter. 'Why won' you fix it?'

A phone call to the Royal Flying Doctor Service in Port Hedland is reassuring. They're impressed, or at least the medical officer says he is, at how competently I'm acting. I don't tell him how I feel. That isn't part of the deal. He tells me they'll have a plane in the air as quickly as they humanly can. I expect nothing less. He tells me he'll ring a respiratory paediatrician at Princess Margaret Hospital for Children in Perth, and ask them to ring me with advice, support and information. I'm grateful. Their backing is valuable, if distant. They're my lifelines to the world of medicine, the world that has become suddenly and frighteningly remote.

'The most important thing is to hydrate the baby,' the doctor reminds me, as if I needed the reminder.

'Can you put in an intravenous drip? Or a naso-gastric tube?' he asks.

'Not a hope,' I say. 'She's too dehydrated; I can hardly feel her pulse, let alone find a suitable vein. And she has no swallowing reflex. The tube would go into her lungs.'

'Mmm,' he murmurs. There's a long pause. Then he says: 'There's a sterile Trocar kit in your cupboard.' He stops.

'A what?' I ask.

'Trocar,' he repeats, then spells it.

'I don't know what that is,' I say helplessly. 'And I don't know how to use it.'

'Oh,' he says. He sounds disappointed. 'Never mind.'

While I talk on the phone, the crowd spills into the office. I hold the baby tightly against me. The air is becoming increasingly stuffy, in spite of the refrigerated air-conditioning. Neither of the health workers is at work because it's Saturday. I haven't had time to ask about them. On this of all days I would have appreciated their company, assistance and input.

'Does anyone know where Joannie and PW are today?' I ask, not singling anyone out for an answer.

The women shuffle, shifting their weight from foot to foot. No one answers and I don't pursue my line of inquiry. It *is* Saturday, their day off, I remind myself.

'I want someone to get Sandy,' I say. Sandy won't mind if I ask her to help.

'I will, Sis,' says the woman standing closest. She's holding a little boy in her arms.

I pull the baby and the blanket closer, and sitting at the desk, I scribble:

'Come quickly, please.' I sign the note and look up. The boy puts his hand out to take the paper. I hesitate.

'This is really important,' I say to no one in particular.

'Really important,' a couple of women echo solemnly.

'That's a'right, Sis,' says the mother of the child. 'Give it to him. He wants to carry it for you.'

'Please make sure you give it to Sandy. No one else,' I say, feeling helpless.

An hour later, the coordinator's wife saunters in.

'Came to see what the commotion was,' she says. 'There's been a lot of talk, but no one was making sense.' She looks around, takes in the bizarre scene. 'Why didn't you send for one of us?'

I don't explain. I must have sweated litres under the blanket, but it isn't until I see her that I discover my mouth is parched and my head aches from lack of fluids.

'Please get me something to drink, water, anything, quickly. And then can you act as a traffic warden to sort out this crowd?'

'Sure,' she says, disappearing. She returns with a glass and a jug of tap water. 'I'll put some ice in it in a minute,' she says. 'But you look desperate for a drink. I didn't want to waste time with it.'

The water's only slightly warm and I spill it down the front of my shirt as I gulp greedily, not pausing to say thanks. I've forgotten how good water tastes.

'Now, then,' she says. 'How do you feel about me working in the clinic? Nothing too clever, but I can manage simple first aid.'

'Go for it,' I say gratefully. 'Then I can concentrate on the baby.'

I resuscitated the baby girl again before the plane came and I handed her over to doctor and nurse. By the time she was safely on the plane, I was exhausted but triumphant. The next morning, I found the note asking for help, where it had blown after the child had let it go, hard against the fence outside the clinic.

The baby was flown to the intensive care unit at Princess Margaret Hospital for Children. Longing for news of her, I rang each morning until she was returned to Jigalong.

'She's got pneumonia,' her paediatrician told me. 'But we can't work out what's going on. The pneumonia isn't severe enough to have made her so dramatically ill.'

Later I heard a cautionary tale. Another young woman had conceived a baby 'wrongly'. The father was a man she should not marry, because they were not the right skin. That baby also was taken to the children's hospital because he was acutely ill, and he recovered. Later, his family took him to an outstation, where he was accidentally dropped on his head, and later died. The Martu men said there was no use in crying about a baby like that. They said it had no spirit. Because he'd been conceived wrongly, he couldn't live.

My third call to the Royal Flying Doctor the following afternoon was a tame affair after all the excitement of Saturday. The patient was a man who'd previously been treated in Perth. He suddenly became too ill to stay home and needed urgent hospitalisation, but not dramatic emergency care. I reassured him, gave him oxygen and drove him to the airstrip as soon as we heard the plane. By the time we got there it was circling overhead.

'Three times in two days!' the medical officer commented with a grin. 'I hope you are not developing a habit!'

I watched with relief as the man climbed into the plane. It was as if the universe had presented me with a weekend-long role test — one I'd passed, if not with flying colours, then at least without losing too much face or any lives.

14

A day or two later, I met Jim Marsh outside the store. He'd been one of the guests at the barbecue and we'd chatted briefly then, but he'd gone home to Darwin the day after Margaret left. He was a linguist, one of the few researchers who had worked consistently at Jigalong. For years he'd been going in and out of the settlement, and had written a Martu Wangka dictionary. He had the confidence of the Jigalong community and had developed close friendships with many Martu families. He interpreted not only the language but also the customs, values and behaviour of the Martu in ways that made my work more manageable. A sensitive mentor, he rescued me from some of my worst faux pas.

'Would it be helpful if I told you some things that might help you?' Jim offers one day.

'I'd like that, please. I feel very lost.'

'Yes, I've been watching you.'

'Come to the clinic where we'll be cool. We can have a cold drink while we talk,' I say, wanting to postpone this discussion. I'm apprehensive about what he might tell me.

Jim waits until I've poured lemonade into glasses and sit opposite him at the table.

'What I'm going to tell you isn't criticism,' he says, waiting until I nod that it's all right to go on. 'It's just ... the customs here are different from any you're used to.'

'I feel nervous,' I admit. 'I'm scared to think that I've behaved badly.'

'There's no need. No one knows how to act when they first come across a different culture, especially when they're plunged right into the deep end for the first time. It's taken me years of observation to know how things are done at Jigalong.'

'I'd like to learn as quickly as I can.'

'It doesn't work like that. It's a slow process.'

I'm embarrassed. How arrogant of me to imagine I'll be able to master in a short time what it has taken an expert twenty years to achieve. I nod again, but keep quiet, hoping Jim hasn't noticed how conceited I sound. I don't want to offend him.

'One thing I've noticed is that you just walk up to people,' he continues. 'You walk into their camps and knock on their doors. That's not how the Martu folk do it. They wait until they're invited.'

'I don't know any other way to attract their attention,' I say defensively. As a community nurse in the city, people had made me feel welcome. Often, they'd be waiting for me, and the door would open before I had a chance to knock. Often, too, the kettle would be boiling, and there'd be cups and biscuits set out in the kitchen. I expected it to be the same at Jigalong.

'You don't need to attract attention,' he smiles gently. 'These people watch you. They see you coming. They know where you are all the time. You're a stranger. They see you intruding on their space, and they don't like it.'

'You're saying I need to learn my place?'

'Yes. It'd help if you could relax a bit. You could wait casually, about twenty or thirty metres from the people you want to talk to, even when you can see them sitting outside their houses, watching you. There's no hurry. No one's going anywhere. Just wait politely, not looking at them or being anxious. After a while, they'll invite you to come closer, and you can approach them.'

'Why haven't *they* told me that?'

'I expect they don't know how. They wouldn't want to hurt your feelings. They're kind people, and they probably experience your directness as abrasive.'

'You ask too many questions,' he tells me another time. 'It's not the proper way, to pry.'

'I don't think I pry, exactly,' I say. 'And anyway, how will I find out what I need to know?'

'You'll find out in good time. That's if people think it's important for you to know their business.'

'But health *is* my business. It's what I'm here for. What I'm paid to do.'

'In Western culture, that's true,' he agrees, 'and in the context of the Health Department. But Jigalong's different. You aren't in your own culture. Maybe there's some other way?'

From then on I tried, often without success, to recognise and respect the boundaries between the cultures. Sometimes it was impossible because diagnosing disease or even deciphering the symptoms of someone who was acutely ill meant that I needed to ask specific questions. Doctors at the RFDS base and consultants in teaching hospitals would have laughed if I told them I hadn't been able to assess a patient properly because I couldn't ask questions. Working the way Jim suggested was a skill to be practised and internalised. It was unfamiliar behaviour for a woman like me, and I had had no idea that direct questioning was inappropriate in some other cultures.

In time, though, I learned to respect the Martu way, and worked hard at not asking questions unless it was imperative I should know and specifically related to my work. Jim was right.

When they were around, the health workers (and several other women who befriended me) explained what I needed to know, not only for my work, but also about customs and values. As time went on, this included a little about customary law so that I began to see a fuller picture.

15

'Lots of old fellas in Jigalong, eh,' Joannie says. Work in the clinic has been slow for the last hour, and we're cleaning the storage cupboards. It's a task I've been itching to tackle since the day I arrived.

'Yes, I've seen some of them,' I reply, thinking she's making polite conversation.

'You should go to old people's camp,' she suggests tactfully.

'It's not on my list,' I say, consulting the dog-eared page I pull from my pocket. 'Tell me about it.'

'Where the old fellas live. They sometimes too sick to walk to clinic. Margaret goes there most days.'

'Is it far away? Can I walk?'

'Over there. Near the hill.' She nods in the direction of a low rise I haven't noticed before and would never have called a hill, well past the houses on the other side of the road. 'Yo, walk. They waiting for you.'

'What happens about the clinic when I'm not here?'

'We'll look after it. We'll come and get you if you're needed.'

The old people lived in makeshift shelters constructed from rusty iron, hessian and canvas. About fifty dogs, all varieties of mongrels, dingoes and dingo-crosses, circled the camp, snapping and growling protectively. After the first visit, I tried not to go there without a younger person I could rely on to control the animals.

There wasn't a dog in the settlement I trusted. After several encounters I began to shout and make loud guttural sounds in the back of my throat — noises copied from the Martu people — that deterred the animals. If I bent to pick up a rock from the ground, they became quiet and hung back. I rarely had to throw a stone, but holding one in my hand felt powerful. After I was nipped on the ankle, I became even more vigilant. It wasn't a severe bite, but I learned a valuable lesson about being super-alert for dogs that crept soundlessly from behind. I had expected their owners would be offended when I yelled at their animals, but they seemed to approve and even to encourage me. On occasions when I'd been particularly vocal, they laughed.

Discarded cars had been dumped on the incline over the years and sat rusting, forming an almost solid backdrop to the shanties. Visitors sometimes used the car bodies as shelters, adding their own home comforts and making campfires. Other visitors preferred to set up camp near their relatives in the vehicles they'd driven from outstations and other communities, and yet others simply moved into often already overcrowded houses shared generously with a circle of friends and family.

There was no toilet in the old people's camp and only one tap. Under the tap was a constant scummy puddle, a basin formed in the ground from spills and leaks and drips. Often the tap was left running full bore, and sometimes I saw old people urinating and defaecating a few metres away. For people with arthritis and general debility, the ablution block was too far to walk, even if there had been any guarantee that the plumbing would be functioning when they got there. Less than two hundred kilometres from a major wealth-creation centre, these old Australians lived without sanitation in conditions as squalid and impoverished as those in any Third World shanty town.

My visit consumed the best part of the morning. I remembered my manners and waited for each person or couple to acknowledge me before I approached. I drove to the camp at least five times a week after that, and more often if someone was ill or if I wanted to make sure particular old men or women were taking their medication.

One old man who was severely dehydrated lay on an old blanket, barely moving. He refused to come to the clinic, refused anything I suggested except water from the refrigerator that I delivered in lemonade bottles a couple of times a day. He was reluctant at first but, after I badgered him gently, he agreed to sip small amounts, until he was able to drink properly. On the fourth day, I saw him out with his dog, as if he'd never been ill.

While he was sick his wife, almost as old and frail as he, constantly made and remade their camp and rearranged their meagre possessions. She moved everything two or three metres in different directions. Each time I went to the camp, the entrance was in a different location. Even the poor old man was not allowed to rest in one place.

'That old woman has to do that to put the Spirits off the track,' Joannie explained. 'If they saw footprints leading into the same place all the time, they'd be able to follow that old man easily.'

Afterwards, I watched more closely, and saw the other old people also all moved house constantly.

Architects from some government department visited Jigalong.

'We're planning to build an aged care place,' one of them said. 'A permanent structure, where these old people can be cared for properly, not left out in the backblocks to rot.'

Some of the old people he referred to belonged to a generation who had once dwelled as nomads in the desert. They could not live in a fixed, semi-permanent position for fear of the Spirits of their Ancestors; they were unable to cope with being enclosed by rigid walls and a roof.

When a Martu person died in a hut or house, the building was ceremonially smoked to ensure the Spirit did not linger, and then abandoned. These places were occasionally reoccupied, but not until several years had elapsed and the buildings had been repaired and repainted. Constructing accommodation similar to the aged care facilities built in Australian suburbs did not seem a good option for the old people of Jigalong.

When I told the architects my reservations about their project, one of them said: 'Yeah. We've heard that before, Maureen. But it's out of our hands. The decision's been made higher up. Our job is to make it happen, not to buck the system.'

The old folk sat around, sociably minding each other's business in a way I found disconcerting, but which they seemed to enjoy. My white, middle-class values dictated that health care was personal and should be provided in privacy. But they were solicitous of each other and nobody appeared concerned that I discussed their problems, as well as I could given the language and cultural barriers, in front of an audience. After a while, they welcomed me with smiles and laughter and bubbles of language that sounded encouraging, even though I didn't understand the words.

16

Another morning, when the first rush in the clinic has subsided, Joannie directs me on another mysterious errand.

'You should go to the kitchen, too,' she says simply.

'The kitchen?' I echo. I'm beginning to repeat everyone else's statements so often I feel I've lost my own voice.

'Yo. Where they cook the old people's lunch. Behind the store. You've passed it lots of times.'

'If I've passed it, I don't remember,' I say defensively.

'Margaret goes there every week. She likes to see,' she says, as if that makes it mandatory.

No one else has mentioned a kitchen, although I've been here a few weeks. Because I haven't heard about it officially, I'm not even sure if I have a role there, in spite of Joannie's assertions. My confidence has increased a little but in spite of that I can't help wondering about other surprises that may be in store for me. Perhaps there's a hidden time bomb ready to explode?

'Joannie says I should go to the kitchen,' I tell Sandy later, in the community office. 'What should I know about it?'

'One of the coordinators set it up a while ago, to make sure the old people had at least one proper meal a day,' she says. 'It's partly funded by money from the government. What else do you want to know?'

'How it works,' I say. 'Why Joannie thinks I should be involved.'

'It's open for lunch five days a week. The women who run it are paid to work there, but the ingredients they use are bought from the Aged Pension payments.'

'I don't understand. I thought people in the community were paid by cheque.'

'Technically, that's true. But we hold back some of the money when we cash the cheques.'

'Is that legal? To withhold payments, I mean.'

'I don't know about legal. That's how it's been done since I got here. No one's ever questioned it.'

'Perhaps the coordinator should make some inquiries. It's probably classed as elder abuse, to withhold payments of Aged Pensions.'

'Yes, perhaps. But if we keep back the cost, the old people are guaranteed something to eat at least once a day, which is more than they might get if their families had access to all their money.'

It's late morning when I arrive at the building behind the store. I arrange myself in what I hope is a nonchalant fashion about thirty metres away, as Jim Marsh suggested. There's nothing to sit on or lean against. I want to be noticed rather than to fade into the background, so sitting on the ground doesn't seem appropriate and, anyway, I don't want to wear dirty clothes for the rest of the day. I stand there, feeling out of place and self-conscious, like Pooh Bear whistling and trying to look unconcerned while he waits for Christopher Robin to notice him. I have to remind myself there's plenty of time, which is just as well, because no one comes in a hurry to rescue me.

A skinny grey-bearded man hobbles along the well-worn path from the old people's camp. There are no laces in his filthy sandshoes and his shorts are held up with a length of fencing wire. He reminds me of the old Nyoongar men who camped with their families at Dog Swamp, an easy walk from my childhood home a few miles from the centre of Perth. There's a big shopping centre there now, with three banks, a service station and a landscaped park with exotic trees and an artificial lake where the natural, seasonal swamp has been contained.

The Nyoongar men cut clothes-props in the bush and sold them door-to-door. The props, sought after by suburban housewives, were long straight branches with forked ends cut from eucalyptus trees. In the days before spin dryers and Hills hoists, women used the props to hold clotheslines full of wet washing up out of the dirt. I think my mother was afraid of the men, although she insisted she wasn't.

'Come inside, quickly, girls,' she'd urge Elizabeth and me when we heard the cry, 'Props!' or saw the men in our street carrying the poles across their shoulders.

In the noonday Jigalong sun, the old man carries a stout stick grown shiny with long service, which he uses frequently as a crutch while he rests and catches his breath. On his head he wears an Akubra, much favoured at Jigalong, a reminder of the days when Martu men worked as stockmen on their own or neighbouring cattle stations. The hat is battered and dusty, like the rest of him. A dog of dubious age and parentage trots at his side, its ribs showing under its mangy yellow coat. The animal goes ahead three or four metres, turns and runs back, its plumed tail moving regally from side to side. Man and dog look comfortable together, old trusted friends.

Another couple of similar age and attachment joins them. The old men exchange gruff greetings and walk together in silence. The dogs sniff around, familiar. When younger, they probably would have romped and chased each other, but age and arthritis have taken their toll. The men seem not to have noticed me. They stop, lean their sticks against a star picket post, fumble with the buttons of their flies and dribble urine onto the ground in an act of male bonding. Their progress is slow, but in their own time they reach the area in front of the kitchen.

The kitchen was built in the middle of the settlement, behind the workshop and the store. The building is constructed of rusty but substantial corrugated iron. For some reason it's perched high on stilts, a landmark in the flat country. The ramp to the only door is steep, and those risers that have not been lost flap loose. The handrail wobbles. Slats, meant to hold the rail steady, jut out instead at wild angles.

The old men crouch silently in the shade of the building, squinting out at the landscape. The old woman with the toothless grin and crusted eyes, whom I recognise from my first visit to the store, joins them. This time, she's topped off her layers of filthy skirts and a checked flannel shirt with a yellow plastic sou'wester that would once have kept some schoolchild dry. She screeches at the men, kicks out at one of the dogs that ventures too close, and cackles. The men ignore her with studious dignity until she shuffles forward and thrusts her own face close to the face of one of the men, trying to attract his attention. He pushes her away with his elbow, using enough force to make his meaning clear without hurting her, and she wanders a few metres away, where she lowers herself laboriously and sits cross-legged on the hot sand. She places her cracked enamel dish to one side, and coughs and spits vigorously. Then, she carefully smoothes a patch of ground in front of her with her hand and draws in the cleared space. I'm curious about the image she's making, but she's too far away for me to see. Soon, she sits back, ignoring what she's drawn.

Before long, other old men and women arrive, most with dogs at their heels. One woman holds the hand of a tiny girl who skips along beside her. Most of the thirty or more people who assemble are dressed in rags and wear an assortment of boots and thongs. Others have bare feet. The hunters and gatherers of the old order, who once enjoyed the beneficence of their land, now sit or stand around with their enamel and tin and old china plates ready for lunch. There's desultory conversation, but I have the impression there's nothing more they need to say.

The odour of greasy meat, boiling without salt, hangs heavily in the midday sun.

Fifty metres away, young women with babies on their hips, men with cigarettes between their lips, boys and girls playing hooky from school, and adolescents in too-tight jeans go into the store and come out with bags of groceries, pies and sauce, melted ice-creams dripping down their arms, cans of Coca-Cola and ginger beer. They glance without curiosity at the old men and women. One or two of the young ones shout a greeting, but most are intent on their own pursuits and ignore the old people. Food wrappers, plastic bags, Popsicle sticks and empty cans litter the ground where they've been thrown among the dog turds.

I'm deciding what I should do next when a plump woman puts her head around the door of the kitchen. She sees me and beckons with her whole hand, fingers to the ground. It's an almost imperceptible movement, one of many I'm starting to recognise, which complements the speech of the Martu people.

'Put in rest of vegetables,' I hear someone say as I get to the top of the wobbly ramp.

Inside, six or seven women stand around with mugs of tea in their hands, taking a break before they begin the next stage of meal preparation.

'Yo. Meat's been boiling long enough. Plenty here,' another says, taking the lid from one of the huge cauldrons to show me. A swirl of steam fills the room and the fatty smell makes me gag. Instead, I pretend to cough.

'You must have been here since early this morning,' I say when I've recovered enough to trust my voice.

'Soon as them kids go to school. I walk with them, come on along here.'

'Me, too. All go together then.'

They would have spent the morning leaning against a wobbly trestle table, gossiping while they peeled and chopped vegetables. A mountain of peel sits in buckets on the floor. A galvanised iron bathtub, probably scavenged from one of the old mission buildings, holds the peeled vegetables.

'Many vegetables, good variety,' someone says proudly.

'Yo, and frozen ones. In packets. From the store,' another voice adds. It is clear these women have learned about Western-style nutrition and take pride in the meals they prepare for the old folk.

'What else are you cooking?' I ask, nodding towards the grease-encrusted stove, where enormous black pots are bubbling, their lids rocking.

'Let me see,' says the leader. She uses her fingers to enumerate. 'Today we put in three legs of mutton, lumps of pork flap, eh, and 'round five-six packets of chicken pieces. That's prob'ly all.'

'Do you decide what you'll buy?'

'Oh, no. The store, they give us stuff. Sometimes old stuff, eh.'

'Past its use-by date?' I ask anxiously. The last thing I want is for all the old people to come down with attacks of gastroenteritis, although most bacteria would be killed by such vigorous boiling.

'Sometimes. Not today, but.'

'Vegetables goin' in,' says a voice. 'Someone grab them kids, quick.' Half a dozen hands pluck tiny children from the floor, and conversation stops while the vegetables are scooped from the bath and thrown in with the meat. Boiling water sloshes over the side as the pots are filled with potatoes, carrots, pumpkin, and five kilos of ice-encrusted, hard-frozen peas. Finally, the bubbling mixture is topped off with three or four finely shredded cabbages. The meal is high in nutritional value, if lacking in culinary finesse.

Someone squeals as the splashing water narrowly misses her hand, but no damage is done. The meat and vegetables are left to boil over high heat and a high volume of steam surges out of the pots.

Toddlers in soggy, black-bottomed nappies are dumped without ceremony back onto the dirty floor, their noses and ears running with green ooze. In a corner under a bench, one little fellow tears up the rotten linoleum and puts it in his mouth. Another sits with a piece of carrot that has fallen on the floor. He chews thoughtfully and spits out tiny bits.

'Stop fighting, you two!' one of the mothers says cheerfully, as she separates small bodies and untangles tiny hands from each other's hair. 'Little buggers!'

Blowflies swarm on the window sills among the bodies of their forebears, and buzz around the children's eyes.

'Nearly time to dish out tucker,' the leader announces loudly. 'Time to serve up,' she adds with a nod in my direction, in case I hadn't understood.

Several women decant the stew into big jugs, ready to take outside to the waiting customers. A child wails and its mother picks him up and puts him to her breast, one foot resting on the opposite knee as she leans her buttocks against the bench, her day's work over. Another woman uses an enormous serving spoon to feed a mouthful of the stew to the baby on her hip. She tastes the stew, blows on it, then gives it to the baby, who pulls a face and spits, splattering the food all over his mother's face. She grimaces, then laughs and replaces the spoon on the table before she calmly wipes her face on the lower edge of her T-shirt, careless of the expanse of plump abdomen she reveals.

Outside, a queue shuffles towards the bottom of the ramp where the women wait with full jugs. One by one, plates are filled. Sitting in pairs and threesomes the old men and women eat appreciatively. It's Monday.

The dogs wait, banished to the outside of the group until it's their turn to lick the plates and fight over bones.

Two young fellows swagger from the store and join the queue. The old people stop eating and watch.

'Give us some,' one of boys demands loudly, holding out a plate in imitation of the old folk. 'There's plenty for everyone, eh.'

Without protest, one of the women pours food from the jug she is holding into the plates. The youths move away, shovelling the food into their mouths as they go.

'Cheeky buggers, them!' the leader comments.

'I'm surprised you gave them the food,' I say, shocked at the threat implicit in their belligerent behaviour.

'Thems make plenty trouble. We too scared.'

'But that's not their food,' I protest. 'What does the Jigalong Council say?

'They say, "They make no trouble if you give 'em what they want".'

As I walk away, I notice, on the edge of the group, an old man hand-feeding his dog with morsels from his plate.

The decision to go to the school was proudly my own, unprompted by either of the health workers. After all, I thought, I had been employed to do the preventative health work in the settlement, and where better to start than in the school, where I felt most at home because of my long association with schools and children.

It is an easy walk from the clinic, and I arrive midway through the morning to find a school like no other I have seen. There are a few students, some at the computers in the corner, others lying on the carpet. A small child sits on the knee of one of the teachers, while she reads to him. The principal greets me enthusiastically, and I explain the purpose of my visit. I hope to find out what screening has been carried out, and to arrange a timetable with him to ensure all the children in the appropriate grades have their vision and hearing tested before the end of the term.

'I hoped you'd come soon,' he says. 'There's a bit of work for you to do here. It's been a long time since the children were screened, because Margaret was so busy with the clinic. But you are very welcome to come whenever you like. Just arrange the times with the teachers.'

He conducts me from room to room, formally introducing me to the three teachers. In one room the teacher's aide has set up a mini clinic, where she spends part of each day syringing the ears of children with ear infections, and patching up grazes and bruises. We make arrangements for her to come to the clinic to restock her dwindling stores, and to have coffee.

Teaching in a school such as this must be hard, sometimes thankless work, especially as none of the teachers speak Martu Wangka, and the children prefer their own language. Mainstream education — writing, spelling, reading and arithmetic in a language not usually spoken — is almost irrelevant to these children. It is no wonder that the way to staff the school is to pay the teachers a generous allowance, and promise them entry into permanent positions when they return to the metropolitan area.

The teachers tell me absenteeism is high; health problems are rife; and everyone thinks of school as a place for little kids and girls, and most of the boys refuse to attend at all after early adolescence. The teachers make no secret of the fact that they are looking forward to the end of term in December when they will all leave Jigalong for the summer holiday, and at least two will not return the next year.

17

Like health care, the economy at Jigalong was fraught with contradictions. The very old people had little understanding or sense of the value of their Aged Pension payments. Younger people had grown up with a money economy that paralleled and intermingled with the traditional culture of reciprocal relationships. The rest were somewhere between these extremes.

Since they'd had access to vehicles — those that belonged to the community or those privately owned — Martu residents had become highly mobile. They could move around Western Australia, sometimes driving hundreds or even thousands of kilometres to attend cultural events. They also visited towns, where the seduction of hotels, shops, petrol stations and takeaway food outlets would be difficult to resist. They bought vehicles, food, clothes, radios and television sets, not for the status such purchases might have provided, but for their utilitarian and entertainment value. When the money was gone, then everyone had a lean time until the next payday.

Younger men and women knew some of the things they could do with money; but they also lived in a culture where no one had exclusive ownership of anything, so that no one could save enough to buy high-priced items. Those who had money shared with those who had none. This situation led to creative solutions, in the way that colonised people often solve problems imposed by the dominant society. The younger people sometimes spent money in a manner never intended by the Department of Social Security and which could be criticised by the wider society. To an outsider it looked as if some of the young people might have been stealing from the older folk. But what seemed like financial abuse of the aged was simply another manifestation of the differences between cultures.

On days when Social Security payments were made and the cheques arrived, the office staff gave cash to those entitled to it, in exchange for their signatures or marks. People gathered in small groups on verandahs or in scraps of shade next to buildings. Some of the younger men and women visited the old people in their camps. Packs of playing cards came out of pockets, and money changed hands until it was all redistributed. Learned on cattle stations or in homesteads, gambling was a source of fun and diversion across the settlement. Card-playing groups joked and laughed, regardless of who was winning or losing.

'Got big bills,' one man tells me. 'Vehicle's broken down, eh.'

'Too bad,' I sympathise.

'Yo. Cost $6000 to get 'er back on the road.'

'That's a lot of money for repairs. You'll have to work hard, save for a long time.'

'No, Sis. I'll play poker with the old people on Thursday.'

Two days later he's back in the clinic.

'Did it,' he says.

'Did what?'

'Got money, like I told you. They had a good time. I'm going to Port Hedland to see some people about m'vehicle. Soon, eh.'

Taking the money wasn't a problem for anyone. This man needed it and he'd won it, fairly or through his cleverness. He'd provided a few hours of entertainment, much as a volunteer might call a game of Bingo in an aged care facility. The old people weren't harmed; they were sharing their temporary wealth; he would share with them if he had something they wanted or needed. They'd enjoyed the time they'd spent with their own or someone else's grandson, playing poker and other games, even if they didn't fully understand the rules or the stakes.

After a short time, I'm included in some of these reciprocal relationships.

I walk to the store in my lunch break and pay six dollars for half a dozen apples. They're fresh and crisp, the best fruit I've seen for many weeks. I buff one on my sleeve, admire the red, shiny skin. I eat the apple, dawdling on the way back to the clinic, savouring the sweet odour in my nostrils and the way the tart juice fills my mouth when I bite the firm flesh. I put the rest carefully in the clinic fridge, to take home and enjoy later.

During the afternoon a visitor to the clinic investigates the contents of the fridge. He spots my apples and ceremoniously hands one each to his wife and two kids and bites into one himself. I'm challenged to rethink old concepts of generosity and hospitality. I realise that, in my world, they hinge on issuing and accepting invitations rather than sharing freely, without question. I'm too attached to things.

Another day, I discover I have a new neighbour.

'Can I borrow your broom, please, Sister?' asks the woman standing on the verandah when I come back from a trip to the old people's camp.

'Um, why do you need my broom?'

'Because I don't have one,' she says reasonably. 'I'm cleaning up.'

'That makes sense. Where do you want to take the broom?'

'Come and see.'

I follow the woman to a rusty tin shed set well back from the road and adjacent to the health compound. It's one of the many derelict buildings around, and it's the size of a double garage.

'I've never even noticed this building,' I say.

'It's been empty for a long time. I might as well use it. It'll make a good camp,' the woman replies.

'Who does it belong to? Do you have to ask permission to use it?'

'Belongs to everyone,' she says firmly. 'I'll just move in.'

She's managed to prise open the door and move a pile of old timber and other rubbish to the back of the shed to clear an area where she plans to live with her disabled son and anyone else among her kinsfolk who might need a place to stay. When we've swept the floor to her satisfaction, she takes mattresses and pillows from the old station wagon parked outside the door of her new home. She puts them in a pile, but within a few seconds her son has pulled the pile apart and scattered the bedding.

'Come to the clinic, and I'll make you a cup of tea,' I say.

'That would be nice. I haven't made a fire. I'll bring my boy.'

'Of course.'

Inside the clinic, I put the kettle on and go to retrieve a packet of sweet biscuits hidden in a store cupboard for a special occasion. Like everything else, biscuits left in the kitchen are eaten as soon as they appear. The only way I have a reliable source is when I remember to lock them away.

The boy runs from room to room, turning on all the taps. Water splashes over basins and sinks, and his mother chases him and turns off the taps. He turns them on again, faster than she can catch him. After a short time, I distract him with sweet tea and orange cream biscuits while my new neighbour and I talk.

As a very little girl, she had been taken from her family at Jigalong to one of the missions in the south-west. At fourteen, she was brought back as a domestic worker on a Pilbara cattle station, and when her only son was born she came home to Jigalong.

Over time, we developed a friendship that included an understanding about the cleaning utensils and anything else my neighbour wanted to use, an arrangement that fitted the model of sharing I was learning. She wasn't at all fazed, if she'd even thought about it, that everything in the clinic belonged to the Health Department. None of it was mine to share or to lend but, as she considered the clinic my domain and she was my friend, she deduced that everything there was available for sharing. She and her son, and anyone else who was staying with her, used the shower and toilet on the end of the back verandah of the clinic, and most of the time she managed to turn off the taps before they went home. Sometimes it didn't work out like that.

One day, after they had gone home, I opened the door and an accumulation of scummy water rushed out, drenching my shoes and ankles, flooding across the verandah and onto the path. The toilet had been blocked with a T-shirt stuffed in the bowl and forced into the S-bend; cakes of soap blocked the outlets of the shower and basin. All the taps were on full bore. I thought about mentioning it to the boy's mother, but knew such tactlessness would hurt her.

'Cup o'tea?' was her regular greeting when I visited her camp. Often she'd make damper, too. Traditionally, damper was made from plain flour, salt and water, mixed by hand in a big bowl, kneaded, formed into the shape of a flat loaf, and baked in the ashes of the campfire. My neighbour used self-raising flour and sometimes a cup of milk to make a damper that resembled a large, delicious scone. When it was cooked, we scraped the ashes and burnt bits from the loaf and ate it from a communal plate, with butter and golden syrup that melted and ran over our fingers and dripped onto the ground. In spite of the difficulty of caring alone for her son, or maybe because of it, she was a wise woman, full of pain and patience. I enjoyed her company. She and I shared things; we had a bond.

18

Gradually, the tempo of my life changed. Less flustered and more at ease, I had time to reflect that my frantic busyness, imposed by a combination of factors over which I felt I had no control, contrasted with what I saw of the lives of the Martu people. Like most nurses (and many other middle-class, middle-aged individuals) I was committed to the concept of *chronos*. My time was measured by the ticking of watches and clocks, marks against appointments in a diary and the turning of the pages of the calendar.

Work and leisure were counted in units of time into which activity was crammed according to pre-arranged schedules. There were goals to be set and achieved and tasks to be completed within precise time frames. Everything had a starting point and an end point. Life was about being busy, doing things, achieving. *Chronos* has an order, a rhythm and a predictability that's both comforting and comfortable when it is part of one's culture. It is quantative, and what most native speakers of English mean when they talk about time.

The Martu people, on the other hand, appeared to live mostly within *kairos*, a concept of time best described as qualitative. *Kairos* is nebulous. It can't be measured or quantified, and there is no equivalent word in English. Time is indeterminate. It's a moment during which something, or nothing, happens. It's a space in which to be, rather than to do. Timetables are irrelevant in *kairos*, which is why Westerners who don't comprehend often feel frustrated when Aboriginal people don't adhere to timetables, don't always attend appointments on time, and miss meetings altogether.

In some circles the concept of *kairos* is understood as 'God's time'. In this religious sense, the word is frequently employed to describe a period of confusion; a time of disruption in which the old rules no longer work the way they once did; values and norms are challenged; old ways of thinking and doing things become irrelevant. As the *kairos* of the community disturbed my accustomed *chronos*, the grounds on which I'd based my daily living shifted precariously.

The store, school and office that opened and closed at predictable times partially superimposed *chronos* on the more relaxed existence of earlier nomadic lives. But men and women often waited with apparent disregard for the passage of minutes or hours. They sat peacefully, calmly, and if what they were waiting for didn't eventuate they went away, still serene. Groups of people hung around in small patches of shade, passing the time and enjoying each other's company, waiting for the next, unpredictable event. Then, without warning and with no signal I could decipher, they'd move together without a word towards some new activity or place.

At first, I thought the people who came to the clinic at all hours of the day and night, seven days a week, didn't understand about clock time. But over the decades, most Martu had come to understand clock and calendar time. The published timetable stated the opening hours of all the services in the settlement. The clinic was open longer hours than the others and except for medical emergencies, health care was not supposed to be available at other times.

I'd broached this with Margaret before she left.

'You're right,' she said. 'I've often thought about sticking to the proper opening hours. But everyone likes the nurse to be on call. Being strict about opening times would cause more trouble than it'd be worth.'

Alone, I considered being more disciplined but decided that if I tried to change there'd be resistance from the community. It would be disruptive for patients, who'd complain about me among themselves and to the Council. They'd continue to come when it was convenient for them, and if I refused to see them I'd be shamed. In any case, even if I succeeded, Margaret probably wouldn't approve. She'd return to her way as soon as she came back, putting me at odds with the community and with her.

Still deliberating on these problems, I discovered I had time for leisure.

The accountant's wife, Sally, had stocked a room off the side of the main store as a clothing shop that specialised in jeans and T-shirts of the type favoured by the adolescents and young adults in the settlement. Among the more practical clothing, Sally placed trays of trinkets and earrings, and hung bags and hats and headbands from hooks overhead. She'd brought back cotton sarongs from a holiday in Bali, and these were displayed on the walls, filling the place with colour and movement. It wasn't the type of shop I'd generally frequent but it was fun to look, and I enjoyed chatting to Sally. There was no air-conditioning and the heat in the small space ensured I never stayed more than a few minutes.

'Come over to our place on Saturday afternoon,' she invites one day. 'We're having a pool party.'

'How wonderful,' I enthuse. 'I'd love to come. I had no idea anyone had a pool.' I am exhilarated already by the idea of diving into cold water.

'Bring a plate. It's a proper Australian party,' she says with a laugh. 'It's too hard to prepare afternoon tea when you never know what's going to be in the store or who is coming. It's easier if everyone brings something.'

On Saturday, I cross the street to the house where Sally and Ian live with their daughter. I can't see a pool and feel foolish, dressed in my bathers under shorts when there's no sign of a pool or other guests. I'm sure she'd said a pool party, but I must have misunderstood. How embarrassing!

'Up here!' someone calls as I approach the house. 'You've come to the right place.'

I look up, unsure where the voice is coming from. A grinning face and a pale, waving arm are visible over the top of a water tank that stands on a massive concrete pillar. 'You'll have to climb up the ladders, but it's quite safe,' Sally informs me. 'Leave your clothes and sandals down there.'

Watched from above, I strip off obediently and fold my shorts and shirt and put them near some other piles of clothing lying on a rough bench. I look around for somewhere to put my platter of fragile melting moments, still warm from the oven.

'Bring the plate with you,' my hostess says. 'It'll save you having to come up and down twice.'

With one hand clutching the plate, I climb a ladder to the top of the tank stand, while she watches.

'Now the next one,' she encourages, pointing. 'Just a little to your left.'

I shuffle sideways until I reach the next ladder, a metre or so away from the first. The iron rungs are sharp and hot under my bare feet. As soon as I put my head over the top I see that the 'pool' is a galvanised iron tank about four metres in diameter. It's been cut in half horizontally, and the cut edges rolled inwards for safety. Sitting chest-deep in the clear water under sensible hats are half a dozen of the Caucasian locals, in various stages of dress or undress. They wave and greet me boisterously. In the centre of the water, which is dappled with sunlight, a white plastic table has been anchored to the bottom of the tank with a lump of concrete. The table is covered with a plastic cloth and laden with chips and dips and platters of savouries, glasses, cool drink, and a bottle of wine and two cans of beer in spite of the by-laws.

A fair-haired, freckle-skinned child wearing fluorescent pink bathers and matching goggles dog-paddles in circles.

'Look at me, look at me,' she calls, dodging around the adults' legs.

'Welcome!' says Ian, ignoring his daughter. 'This is how the alternative community celebrates Saturday afternoon in Jigalong.'

Cautiously, I swing my legs over the top of the tank and start down the third ladder. My foot touches the tepid water and I lower myself into it gratefully.

'Well done,' someone applauds.

We sit around making small talk, eating and drinking as if there's nothing at all unusual about this gathering.

'Do you do this every Saturday?' I ask. 'Or is it a special occasion?'

'Every Saturday, unless we go into Newman for the weekend,' Ian answers.

'And when there's no Eagles game on the TV,' someone else adds, reaching across the water to take his beer from the table.

'I'm working on a way to get the television set up here, so we can watch the football in comfort.' People laugh, and Ian adds, 'But these things take time.'

'Everything takes time in Jigalong,' someone explains. 'But we use any excuse to get together.'

A gust of hot wind stops the conversation momentarily while people retrieve hats that have blown into the water. Ian stands up to anchor the cloth on the table more firmly by rearranging the plates and bottles and cans in a different configuration.

'Wow, that's cold!' he says as he sits again in the water and it laps above his waist.

'It's a pity the teachers don't come,' one of the men remarks.

'Yes. I hear they've gone into Newman again. They must have learned from us about weekends at the motel.'

'The new principal likes to keep them under his wing. He thinks we might corrupt his little band,' Sally says. 'They're all very young. For most of them, this is their first appointment after university.'

'That'd be tough, Jigalong as your first school.'

'The bonuses are pretty amazing, so they say, for people who come to a school like this. If they stay long enough, they go back to Perth with guaranteed permanency and a big fat bonus, too.'

The West Coast Eagles football team inflamed passions, stimulated the imagination and united blacks and whites at Jigalong like nothing else could. The team's fortunes were followed with dedication, and flags and streamers waved and fluttered through the settlement. Newly included in the Australian Football League, by the early 1990s the Eagles had captured the hearts of the community.

Crowds gathered around television sets on verandahs and in doorways to cheer the team when it played. Men, women and children wore the yellow and royal blue team colours, sporting striped beanies, scarves and jumpers bought from Sally's store. The woollen clothing signified allegiance in spite of the heat shimmering off the desert. The social life of the community was predicated on how well or how poorly the team played, and whether it won or lost. Everyone had an opinion.

I'd ferried my sons to football matches when they were at school, cutting up oranges for half-time breaks and washing and drying the team's jumpers when it was my turn. I'd barracked proudly when 'our team' was chosen to play in the Little League game in the intervals at adult matches. Apart from that, I hadn't taken an interest in Australian Rules or any other code of football. But at Jigalong, I became a convert, although I could not have named more than a couple of other teams in the league. As long as the Eagles won, I didn't much care who opposed them. I drew the line at wearing a beanie but I did make a ribbon rosette in the club colours. I taped it to the noticeboard outside the clinic and for a day I felt I belonged at Jigalong. But the ribbons were stolen overnight and I didn't get around to replacing them.

A football field had been created on the edge of the settlement, although it took a major act of the imagination to call the patch of baked ground, riddled with potholes, a 'field'. The grader that cleared away the spinifex had gouged large fissures, which had never been filled. At one end, two goalposts leaned dangerously towards each other. At the other end, one goalpost and one point post still stood, and another lay on the ground between them. Barefoot boys and youths kicked footballs up and down, enacting fantasies stimulated by photos of Aboriginal West Coast players that adorned the outside walls of the store. A passing AFL official would not have selected any of the Jigalong boys, but what they lacked in skill they made up for in enthusiasm, even if it was short-lived in the heat.

Twice a week, three or four of us, like the expatriate women I'd met in Bangkok, gathered late in the afternoon for an energetic aerobics session. We met in the biggest room in the clinic, behind the kitchen, a room designated as a group room, hardly ever used for its original purpose.

'I hoped aerobics would introduce the Martu women to enjoyable exercise,' Margaret had lamented in one of our conversations over coffee before she left. 'But they don't come.'

Instead, the class was popular with the teachers and other white women. There was only one Jane Fonda video, and none of us ever thought to replace it or buy a new one. With groans and laughter in about equal proportions, we jumped and ran and contorted ourselves into unnatural postures, all to music and in the name of good health and slender bodies. Invitations to join the class were pinned up in the store, the school and the office. Occasionally, one or two younger Martu women joined us, but their attendance was erratic. They saw no point in our gyrations, or, more likely, they were put off when they saw so many white women.

19

On alternate Thursdays, when there was no doctor's clinic, feeling like an irresponsible parent sneaking respite from children who demanded constant attention, I escaped in the Nissan to Newman. After the two-hour drive, I collected from one of the pharmacies prescription medications that could not be sent on the truck, and went to the hospital to deliver pathology specimens and to visit patients from Jigalong. From the Newman Community Health Centre, I collected mail that might have been sent there. After the first two or three times, I stopped expecting a warm welcome or congenial company. The nurses were kind enough, but they made it clear they were all much too busy to socialise with yet another stranger from Jigalong.

When I'd overcome my anxiety about the solo drive and my confidence behind the wheel had increased, these trips developed an aura of magic. Small pleasures — being alone, thinking without interruption, listening to the regional radio station as I drove — no longer taken for granted as my right, assumed wonderful significance. Hitting graded gravel and eventually reaching the bitumen road was like being in touch with home. On the outskirts of the town, on playing fields surrounded by tall gum trees, vast flocks of white sulphur-crested cockatoos foraged for grass seeds, their usual raucous screeching temporarily stilled. They were unperturbed by the groups of

Aboriginal men and women who often sat or reclined with their flagons of cheap wine under the shade of the trees that bordered the parkland.

Some Martu families had left Jigalong to set up camps and outstations further into the desert so they could live more traditional lives and raise their children away from the influence of alcohol and other disruptions. Another group had been drawn to Newman by the promise of easily accessible alcohol, which could be bought without restriction from the hotel with money from their social security payments. At first they camped in their vehicles on the edge of the town for a day or two. Later, they put together makeshift and semi-permanent constructions, where they camped for longer and longer periods until, eventually, they formed an ongoing group of poverty-stricken fringe dwellers on the edge of the affluent mining town.

For the elders in Jigalong, this would have meant heartbreak. They would grieve to see their younger men and women apparently reject their traditional ways, to be pulled down by alcohol and prostitution. They would worry, also, for the wellbeing of their grandchildren, frequently neglected by their parents, separated from their own people. The elders must have recognised they were powerless to change the situation.

The non-Indigenous residents of Newman tolerated the camp, but not without complaint. When it became clear that a group of Aboriginal people had made Newman their permanent home, the East Pilbara Shire built an ablution block. This gave the camp some sort of legitimacy, because it was seen by many to have the approval of local government. In time it became known as the Pumajina community, although it did not enjoy the status of the communities that had their own administrative councils.

The town benefited from the creation of a permanent campsite. Instead of ignoring the fringe dwellers, the local authorities could monitor the environment and regularly remove rubbish and other health hazards; the hospital and community health services provided efficient health care; welfare services intervened to care for neglected or abused children; and the area could be policed as a way of limiting family and other violence.

To begin with, I was unaware of the Pumajina community.

After the first couple of excursions to Newman, my visits took on a ritual sequence. My first stop after I'd completed the chores was at the only café in town, where I drank a cappuccino and read real news in that morning's paper, a special satisfaction after perusing papers that were at least a week old when they arrived at Jigalong on the store truck. Then I drove to the swimming pool in the centre of the town. This was the focal point of my trip. I swam lap after lap in the clean, clear water, until all the desert dust was washed away and I was recharged. The pool was a sanctuary, a haven in the desert, with palms and shady moist lawns around a body of water that refreshed and revived my often-drooping spirits.

The proximity of the fringe camp created a hiatus in my otherwise blissful breaks. A group of people, often drunk in the middle of the day, kept me under surveillance as I moved around the town and invariably confronted me when I returned to the vehicle after my playtime.

'Give us a lift back to Jigalong, Sis,' blusters a big man I don't recognise. He swaggers too close, barring my way to the Nissan. Half a dozen people close in behind him. They form a tight circle. I'm overwhelmed by the scent of unwashed bodies, tobacco, alcohol fumes. I'm scared.

'Let me into the vehicle,' I say, inching my way through the crowd. Grudgingly, they move away and let me inside. Now they're deliberately menacing, banging on the doors and the roof of the vehicle. I'm unnerved, unsure how many people — others

I can't see — are involved, and their level of sobriety or drunkenness. I pray there's an audience of police officers or miners who might protect me, but no one comes to my assistance.

'This vehicle belongs to the Jigalong community, eh,' someone says insolently. 'You drive us back!' His words are accompanied by violent kicks to the wheels and thumps on the roof.

'No, this is a health vehicle, not a community one. And I don't have to drive you anywhere,' I argue through a partly open window. I feel angry that I have this disagreement whenever I come into town.

The ending is always the same: a string of abuse that includes sexist and racist name-calling, vehemently spat at me in an attempt to control my behaviour. Roughly translated, the tirades indicate that my adversaries think I'm an uncooperative, licentious, overpaid white woman of dubious parentage. They assure me solemnly that someone will punish me properly very soon. If it's not them, it'll be someone they know. My heart thumps as I drive away.

Sometimes people needed non-urgent admission to the hospital. If PW or Joannie were on duty, they drove the patients in one of the clinic's vehicles. PW was businesslike about driving to Newman. I think he enjoyed the change in his working routine, and often brought back passengers. He set off cheerfully, but said little. When Joannie went she made an outing of it, like me.

'Is it OK if I camp out?' Joannie asks one afternoon.

'Of course. That's a good idea. It'll save you driving in the dark tonight,' I reply.

She gathers her sisters and some of their children. I watch, amused, as they bundle into the ambulance the things they'll need overnight: some tucker, maybe; swags, pillows and blankets; a billy or two. They all crowd into the vehicle with an old woman who has a chest infection. Perhaps they'll sleep at the

Pumajina camp, where they'll catch up with friends, or maybe along the road. They seem happy and confident, so I don't worry. There are no seatbelts in the back and I wonder if I'm responsible for the safety of the children, the carload, but I'm not the driver and I'm powerless to stop the excursion now it has started.

In time, I will remember to clean the inside of the ambulance every time it returns, to remove the chicken legs and chips and takeaway food cartons dropped or thrown on the floor, and the Coke cans and bottles that, unchecked, rolled irritatingly from one side to another under the bunks.

On weekends when someone needed to be driven to hospital, I would ring Sandy. Before I loaded the patient into the back of the ambulance, I'd run to the flat and gather a hat and my purse, as well as my bathers and towel. I'd fill a container with four litres of drinking water in case of a breakdown. To be without water in the desert would be a disaster too terrible to contemplate. With Sandy for company, I'd drive to the hospital. Sometimes it took all the discipline I could muster, in my impatience, to complete the formalities and hand the patient over to the ward nurses.

Then, like schoolgirls let out to play, Sandy and I would head for the pool, to the café, to a takeaway outlet. Still in our bathers, we would drive back to Jigalong, eating chicken or fish and chips as we went.

20

Joannie sits with me on the verandah. We're waiting until it's time to put away the paraphernalia of another working day and lock up the clinic, on one of the rare occasions when there's no one demanding our attention. We could have gone home earlier, but it's companionable here, and neither of us is in a hurry. The sun has lost its sting; the warmth is comfortable on my bare arms. If the evenings get much cooler, I'll have to unearth a tracksuit. There's a soft apricot glow, and shadows from the two dusty, stunted tamarisks growing by the back fence slant across the path. They'll be covered in sprays of pink and white flowers when the rains begin. Planted by some missionary over half a century before, they've survived the blistering heat of arid summers and the onslaught of wanton children and feral goats. The feathery branches scarcely shade the ground beneath them.

Joannie's child, a toddler in a faded blue dress with a torn hem, squats flat-footed on the warm ground in front of us. When she moves, I see she has no nappy. It shouldn't surprise me that the little girls and old women in the settlement suffer so much from urinary tract infections. They sit without pants on the ground, where generations have spat and vomited, urinated and defaecated. I imagine myriad bacteria in the dust, lying quietly, predators that wait for a moist host to invade, where they can grow and multiply.

Joannie runs her long, strong fingers through the hair of one of the teenagers who came to the clinic to be entertained in air-conditioned comfort when the sun was high and the day hot. They had asked, giggling, heads hanging, feet shuffling, if they could watch a video from the resource library, the small collection of books and teaching aids that's been acquired randomly from marketing catalogues over the years. There has been a succession of community nurses who've passed through the clinic, each one filling in request forms in triplicate for new acquisitions, in the hope that the women and men would be 'educated' about health matters. I'm happy to let the girls watch the videos. It's part of my plan to encourage people to expand their use of the clinic, and not to see it only as somewhere to bring the ill and injured.

One of the girls sitting with us has an older sister who is pregnant. The expectant mother, flanked by a group of her young friends, comes often to watch the video that depicts the birth of a baby in simple, graphic images and language. At first, they were embarrassed. They giggled and nudged each other, and whispered behind their hands. But after the first couple of times, they sit without talking. As they watch, they dunk biscuits in the coffee they slop all over the floor and down the front of their T-shirts.

The girls are shy. They're far too private to engage in conversation about a confronting video. Or, rather, a video they might have found confronting half a dozen viewings ago. By now, I think they could recite the soundtrack verbatim, complete with the nuances and inflections of the professional actors who portray the labouring woman, her husband and the array of non-Indigenous midwives and educators who point to diagrams and explain, in earnest voices and great detail, the process of labour in a delivery ward in a hospital. The time for discussion has long passed.

The younger girl sits at Joannie's feet on the rough concrete.

'Find wingers,' she commands, pointing to her head.

Next to her, an older girl scratches delicately behind her left ear with one finger. At the mention of wingers, my scalp is instantly itchy, too, and I clasp my hands together in my lap to fight the urge to scratch. Joannie complies without comment. I watch as she parts the girl's curls, dividing the hair as she scans each strand for nits. There's an uncomplicated intimacy between them. The girl's dark hair glints red and gold in the afternoon sun.

Joannie hums tunelessly as she works, peering intently, looking for signs of nits bound by adhesive secretions to the shafts of hair.

'All clean,' she pronounces. 'No wingers today.'

She doesn't remove her fingers, but continues to massage the head in front of her with gentle movements. I'm envious of the girl. It's been many weeks since I've felt intentional touch. There's been casual contact — an occasional child who has flung itself into my arms, a baby who has sucked the silver snail I wear on a chain around my neck as a reminder that I am sometimes slow to recognise old mistakes, so all too often repeat them.

The girl rests her head against the knee behind her and closes her eyes. We are companionable, quiet.

A dog barks, not too far away, and the spell breaks. There is good reason to be scared of the dogs and the almost tame dingoes that roam the camp, scavenging for scraps. Nipped on the ankle at the old people's camp, I think I'm lucky not to have been more seriously bitten and perhaps ended up like the three-year-old boy with the mauled face we had to send to hospital on the Royal Flying Doctor Service plane. I look around to locate the source of the noise, hoping there is someone to control the animal. A mangy-looking mongrel pads along the other side of the fence and out of sight.

Joannie shifts her position on the bench. The girls change places on the ground. The older woman examines the second head of hair carefully. When she's finished, she gives the girl a gentle push.

'Will I check yours?' she asks diffidently when the girls have wandered away.

'Please,' I answer. She moves to stand up, and I say, 'No. Sit where you are.' The relationship between us blurs. 'You look comfortable,' I tell her. 'I'll sit on the ground.'

I want to be like the girls, and feel her hands in my hair, fingers against my scalp. I take out the scrunchie I wear to keep my hair off my neck and out of my eyes, and shake my head to loosen my hair. As I do, I smell shampoo and conditioner and the sweat of the day. I sit at Joannie's feet, wriggle to adjust my back against the bench between her spread knees, and she begins.

She is thorough. I feel her part my hair methodically like a hairdresser from the crown of my head to the base of my skull, then divide each strand again, as she did with the girls' hair. She picks up each section, and replaces it. I relax, enjoying the sensation and the rhythm of her movements. She pauses. I feel her separate one or two hairs and run her index finger and thumb along the shaft, pulling slightly. She says nothing.

I worry.

'Did you find one?' I ask, trying to hide my anxiety.

Her fingers move again, purposefully. She is silent.

'No,' she says finally. 'No nits.' Her hands are still, resting in my hair. 'That come out too easy. Nits are too hard.'

I worry about what I'd do if I did have nits. They are baseless, useless worries, of course. There is a box full of Quellada lice and nit treatment in the cupboard and I can take a bottle and shampoo my hair with it in the privacy of my flat. But old shame fills my thoughts, whispered stories about children being banished from school because they had lice, and the stories told by my mother and grandmother about children at their schools having their hair shaved. Shaved! The idea fills me with horror.

In those days, there were only cutthroat razors, which were terrifying enough. Then bare scalps were doused in kerosene, with no regard for cuts and nicks in the skin. Those were the old remedies. Joannie knows about them, too. She's told me stories of children brought to this very place when it was a mission, and treated like lepers because they had nits.

'Not a medical problem,' I'd once heard a school nurse say. 'This is a social problem.'

All the more reason to be afraid. My own scalp tingles with fear.

I take a deep breath, determined not to lose the moment. I lean back again and will myself to enjoy Joannie's touch in my hair. She's stopped humming. I can hear her breathing softly, in and out through her mouth.

'Your daughter plays quietly,' I say, watching the child. 'She amuses herself.'

The child looks up and I say her name. She watches us for a moment and then continues her game with a handful of bottle tops and some ants that have strayed onto the path.

Joannie brings the child with her most days. At first I thought it strange that she'd interrupt her work to attend to her daughter when she needed attention. But no one who comes to the clinic seems to think anything of the health worker having her daughter with her, and I quickly accepted that things happen differently at Jigalong from how I once thought they should. It is another way of doing things, that is all. Sometimes, she brings her sister's daughter, as well.

'It's skin,' she says, as if that explains everything.

We are quiet. I'm learning about 'skin' and the complex relationships among the Martu people, which everyone, except me, understands. Even tiny children know how all the other people they come in contact with fit into their lives. They know to share and engage fully with one group, to hold back, reticent with some, and to avoid others completely.

'You have a skin,' Joannie tells me now, as we sit on the verandah in the fading evening light.

I feel confused, suddenly shy. I wonder if I should ask, or wait and be told more. I remember how I've made mistakes when I haven't dealt sensitively with what I'd been told, or when I've gone straight to the heart of a matter with the curiosity of a counsellor. If I have a skin it will mean I have reciprocal social networks and obligations with a particular group of people.

I wait.

'I'll tell you, if you want,' she says, engaging me with her smile.

She looks away. I stare into the distance. I'm waiting for more, wondering what this can mean, about the privileges and obligations involved. I am not sure by what authority she can talk like this to a white woman.

'You are the same skin as me,' she says quietly, naming the skin group to which she belongs.

As if she understands what has happened, the toddler puts her arms out to me, and I lift her onto my lap. She snuggles into me, and touches my snail.

'That will make me an auntie to this child,' I say.

'Yes,' Joannie replies quietly.

I hadn't heard other white people talk about their classification in the kinship system. Touched, I felt close to tears. But it made perfect sense in a society where kinship is the basis of all relationships, absorbed with language from babyhood. If the Martu people were even to talk with me, it would have to be in the context of our social relationship. Joannie and PW and everyone else with whom I came into contact would not have been able to interact with me unless they knew my designated place in the life of the community. They had known all along where I fitted. What was different now was that I knew also. Knowing made it possible for me to find out what my responsibilities were and perhaps to act with more circumspection. I was curious about the classifications of the other white people who lived in the settlement. I wondered whose responsibility it was to nominate the position of strangers, and why only some of us were told and others were not.

The way people behaved made more sense. Relationships between women, on the whole, were less formal than those between men of different classificatory groups. Relationships between men and women were easier to distinguish, ranging from joking at one extreme (between those who could call the other person 'spouse') to a total avoidance relationship. It no longer puzzled me that PW often put his head around the door of the clinic to see who was there. He did not want to encounter women who were in the group he would call 'mother-in-law', which included not only the mother of his wife, but also some other women. On one occasion, presumably a near miss, he ran from the clinic and did not return that day.

It also made sense that some of the men could treat me with easy familiarity, and talk and joke casually, while others were distant, aloof — although if anyone required first aid or health care, my role as a white nurse overrode their need for avoidance.

21

One Thursday morning as I drive out of Jigalong, a middle-aged couple stops me. They stand close to the road and the woman pretends she's about to walk in front of the Nissan. When I stop, she runs around to the driver's side.

'Give us a lift, Sis?' she asks as I wind down the window.

I saw them yesterday at the clinic, after the man's leg had been injured in a fight.

'The other bloke, he 'it me with a tyre lever,' the man had said, pulling up a leg of his tracksuit pants to show me. 'Damned hard. Came down whoosh.' He made a chopping movement with his arms, hands held together. 'It musta broke somethin'.'

The leg was swollen and bruised and he winced when I touched it. Although he was still walking, I suspected he might have a small fracture.

'What happened to the other man?'

'He got away. Drunk bugger!' he laughed ruefully.

'You'll need an X-ray. You'll have to go to Newman, but you can't drive with your leg like that. Can you get him into town?' I asked his wife, not sure if she could drive.

'Yo. Tomorrow,' she said. 'No problem then.' A mobile couple, they travelled around freely, and it was already too late in the afternoon to ask the health workers to drive so far. It would be well after dark before they got home again.

If they hadn't been going to the hospital, I'd most likely have refused to take them with me, which would have been my loss. They entertained and educated me all the way to Newman, and told me about themselves and their country. They pointed out a bungarra and a kangaroo, neither of which I would have noticed if I'd been driving alone. They taught me a few Martu Wangka words, laughing with me because I found them so difficult to pronounce.

'There wile dargies,' the man says, *sotto voce*, pointing with his chin.

I look where he's pointing, but see only the scenery I always see, with no living thing. I roll the syllables around in my head, but it takes a while until I recognise the words.

'Ah, wild turkeys,' I say at last. 'Where? I'll stop so I can see.' I stop the vehicle immediately, on the hump in the middle of the track.

'Over there,' he says, pointing in a slightly different direction now.

I catch a glimpse of movement, too fast to identify as birds.

'They *nyabaru*,' the man adds softly.

'Oh, I'm sorry. I didn't know. Can you tell me why we can't talk about them?'

'Same name as someone else,' he explains, making the familiar rocking motion with his hand.

'Someone who's passed away?'

'Yo.'

As I negotiate the track, I say 'wild turkeys' over a few more times in my mind. Then I remember that the health workers always ask for the *nyabarus* when they want the car keys because, PW once told me, they couldn't say 'Keith', a name he said sounded too much like 'keys'.

The man sits in the back on our return trip to Jigalong, his leg in a heavy plaster cast stretched out along the seat. The woman is in the front, next to me. Suddenly, she orders me to stop.

'We'll get out now,' she says when I pull over. She turns in the seat and addresses her husband: 'You stay here.'

'I don't think he can go anywhere easily,' I say.

She nods at my joke. 'You come with me,' she says.

We walk perhaps thirty metres, back along the way we've just come. The woman stands still and points to a network of large cracks in the compacted ground at the side of the track.

'Look,' she says. 'Bush potatoes growing there.'

'You have sharp eyes,' I tell her. 'I've never noticed cracks like that, and I've come this way often.'

'You weren't looking, that's why, eh? I know how to look. My grandmother taught me when I was a little girl. Plenty of tucker round here.' She inspects the ground, hands on her hips. 'This is the spot where we should dig.' She points precisely with a bare toe at a crack that looks to me like all the others in the desert. 'Pity we don't have a crowbar or a digging stick with us, or we could take a feed back to the mob,' she says.

She's clearly disappointed, but there is nothing we can do and we go back to the vehicle in silence.

'Thank you for such an interesting day,' I say as I stop the vehicle outside their camp and wait while the man climbs laboriously down. 'I hope I'll be able to see animals and birds along the track, now you've shown me how.'

22

Women and children with predictable ailments wander in and out of the waiting room. Toddlers with crusted eyes; babies with runny ears that will yield dead flies to my syringes full of warm water; and children with infectious impetigo — scabby sores oozing pus — play on the floor. An old man with a yellow beard, rheumy eyes and a wheezing chest sits grunting in a corner. He's been slumped there most of the afternoon, escaping the heat.

I watch as he pokes slyly with his stick at an inquisitive toddler who's come too close. With bony fingers, he pinches the cheek of another child. The boy bellows, then retreats to his mother for comfort. She drags him onto what's left of her lap and hugs him close to her pregnant abdomen. She turns her back towards the old man and murmurs an endearment with her mouth close to the boy's ear. The child smiles and squirms around so he can see the old man.

Diabetics, pregnant women and known carriers of sexually transmitted infections present themselves for checks and treatment. On the back verandah, previously lethargic babies splash where I put them, waist deep, in a cool communal bath in the old trough, watched by their amused mothers. The community has minimal understanding of hygiene or health principles. The only person concerned seems to be me, and when it comes to bathing babies together, I manage mentally to minimise the possibility of cross-infection. After all, these kids share their beds, food and clothing. Local families do not have the luxury of baths in their houses; there are few showers and even fewer that work, so a baby playing in water is a novelty. The women take cold drinks from the fridge and occupy themselves while they wait, suckling babies, gossiping in Martu Wangka, and checking each other's hair with practised fingers and sharp eyes for wingers and nits.

The old woman with many skirts arrives at the clinic.

'Give us a skirt, Sis,' she pleads in English I have trouble deciphering.

'But you're wearing three skirts already,' I say, pointing to the layers flapping around her ankles.

'Give us a skirt, Sis,' she repeats as if she hasn't heard me.

I watch her go from person to person in the treatment room, speaking in her own language and cackling. The adults respond good-naturedly; they talk to her and touch her on her hand or arm. But the children hide behind their mothers. She asks me again for a skirt and I realise her mind has wandered back and is stuck in the old days when the missionary nurses would have provided secondhand clothes for the people who camped outside their fences. Now she has some form of dementia.

'We're so busy,' I complain to Joannie as I walk through the treatment room on my way to the next patient. She clatters the metal dishes in the sink and I wonder if perhaps she hasn't heard.

'Why are we so busy? I can't keep up,' I try again, looking to her as an ally.

She shrugs one shoulder, without looking at me, and continues washing up. I'm frustrated and anxious.

'I don't even know half of these people,' I snipe. 'As if anyone cares,' I finish under my breath.

For days, there's been a trickle of Jigalong people returning from mysterious journeys. Newcomers have arrived from the outstations and other communities. The crowd has built up and people camp in old cars and makeshift shelters on the barren rise at the back of the old people's camp. The store, always an attractive gathering place, is packed all day like department stores during their after-Christmas sales.

The younger men are especially rowdy. For hours, several cars have driven laps around the settlement, up and down the single dirt roads, engines revving and horns blasting. The passengers, packed in too tightly for safety or comfort, lean out of windows and yahoo. Groups of young fellows stand on opposite sides of the road and shout at each other. Dogs bark incessantly, adding decibels to the human noise and the confusion.

Outside, the shadows are lengthening. The women with babies in their arms tug at the older children, urging them outside into the stiff easterly wind. The old man levers himself out of his seat and shuffles away, stick in hand, an Akubra hat askew on his old head.

'See you tomorrow,' Joannie says abruptly. 'I gotta go, too.'

Suddenly, the clinic's empty.

I stand at the doorway feeling left out, like a child who knows there's a significant family crisis, a secret no one's willing to share. Everyone appears suddenly purposeful as they leave the clinic, and soon the women and children disappear from the roadway. It doesn't matter, I comfort myself. If I needed to know, someone would tell me. I should have asked Joannie before she left what all this activity means. But I have enough to do without worrying about vague secrets. I'm unsettled, edgy, all the same.

A vehicle with no front bumper and no number plate streams in a dust cloud along the road from town. As it draws level with the clinic, I notice the rusty metal of a crumpled door on the driver's side. The driver swerves to avoid the piles of tyres and, as the wheels spin and gravel splutters behind, the vehicle accelerates towards the middle of the settlement. It narrowly avoids the corner of the cyclone wire fence and speeds past the school. The driver brakes fiercely and the vehicle screeches to a stop outside the workshop.

Men run from everywhere; it's as if they've been waiting for news the driver brings. I watch a small group of elders congregate. They seem to be murmuring or whispering in a tight huddle, their heads close together. The young men who've been so rowdy and disruptive all day stand quiet and still on the edge of the group, subdued in the presence of the elders. They listen and nod with their heads down. Within minutes, the cluster breaks up and all the men wander off, two or three at a time, heading towards the eastern end of the settlement.

The sun is setting over the low hill, a blaze of orange in the dust, as PW knocks imperatively on the wall of my flat, rattling the wire door. His matted hair, in silhouette from the sunset, is more unkempt than usual, and he's breathless from running.

'We need the ambulance now, eh,' he says, his voice a mixture of urgency and diffidence.

'Is someone hurt?' I ask. 'What's happened?'

'No, Sis,' he says. 'No accident. No one's hurt. But we need the ambulance anyway.'

I hold the door open and invite him in, offer tea and biscuits which he refuses with a shake of his head and a quick, dismissive movement of his hand. He acts as strangely as the others in the community today. I try to make sense of his request, acutely aware, yet again, that I'm an outsider. I'm always completely outside the culture and context in this mysterious country and at a time like this I feel out of my depth, too.

PW moves impatiently from one foot to the other on the brown carpet. He's clearly loath to explain the message he's brought from the other elders, and I'm equally reluctant to agree to him taking the ambulance without knowing exactly why he is asking. The behaviour of the men all afternoon, followed by this strange request, has confused me. I recognise my rising apprehension.

I can't name the source of the anxiety, but it has nothing to do with this man wanting to borrow the LandCruiser. It's not as if the health workers don't frequently drive the Health Department vehicles. They're both competent drivers and usually it is *I* who ask *them* to take one of the vehicles on an errand or to transport people. But this request doesn't make sense unless someone's hurt or sick.

'We need the ambulance. Now,' he demands. His voice, as a rule so soft and gentle, is loud and insistent.

'I hear what you are asking,' I say. 'But what do you need it for? You know I can't let you have it unless I know what for.'

He hangs his head. 'To get the body of *Nyabaru* — I cannot say his name,' he mumbles at last. 'From the hospital in town. It's time to bring 'im here for the funeral.'

'I'm sorry,' I gasp. 'I didn't understand. But I don't know about carrying a body in the ambulance. What usually happens?'

PW is becoming even more agitated. 'Margaret always says, "OK". It's what we do.'

With no one else to consult, I agree reluctantly, chary about letting the vehicle go. In my fear I want to control the situation, while at the same time I am unable to explain my trepidation. I put the keys into his hand grudgingly, and listen as he starts the engine and drives quickly through the gates of the clinic compound, leaving them open as he'd found them.

I'd had several puzzling conversations with a clerk from the Newman Hospital about a body they'd been keeping in the morgue, waiting for the Martu elders to arrange a funeral. But there were so many other things that clamoured for my attention that I'd forgotten. Through observation and several guarded conversations with the health workers, I knew that the bodies of

Martu people were not recovered immediately from hospitals, because of Sorry Business occurring in other communities or towns. Death was a taboo subject and it was not proper for anyone to discuss this funeral with me, so I did not know a burial was imminent. Later I will discover that under customary law Martu people have a serious obligation to attend the funeral rituals of people to whom they are related within certain kinship groups. The obligation overrides other responsibilities or commitments they may have, which explains the frequent, previously incomprehensible absences of PW and Joannie from the clinic.

I spend the rest of the evening more than a little troubled. The book I've been enjoying seems remarkably tedious, and I quickly lose interest. The television set emits white noise, and I can't get a picture. Deciding the ambulance will not return that night, I go to bed.

I awake from unsettled sleep hours later, as the cars and trucks and utilities that accompanied the ambulance on its grisly assignment rumble out of the creek bed. I listen as they negotiate the tyre-barrier, and watch the headlights shine through the windows of my flat. The convoy pauses at the gate of the clinic and soon I hear someone drive the ambulance into the carport, front-first.

'It's not PW,' I think. 'He knows to reverse in, so we can lift a stretcher into the back without any trouble.'

Loud voices explode in a mixture of English and Martu Wangka as men who've been in the ambulance climb or fall out. Doors slam.

I lie still, hardly daring to breathe, waiting for what will happen next, but the men hurry away noisily. I get up hoping to find clues, to get some idea about what's happening. The ambulance is in its place and everything seems normal. I wonder if the body is still in the back but there's no way to find out, unless I go outside in the dark, open the rear door, and look.

Rationally, I know there's nothing to be scared of. After all, as a nurse, I've probably seen and cared for many more corpses than most other people would see in a lifetime. During my last stint on night duty before I finished my training, I sometimes worked as an 'extra'. In this relief role, as a senior though not yet registered nurse, I could be sent to any part of the hospital to relieve nurses who were taken ill in the night, or to assist in wards where the workload had become impossibly heavy. With only two or three young nurses in a ward full of acutely ill people, the death of a patient put considerable stress on the staff, and the extra nurse would take responsibility for laying out the body ready for the arrival of the funeral director.

In spite of my familiarity with death, I'm anxious about spending the rest of the night with nothing more than a fibro wall to separate me from where a corpse lies in the LandCruiser, especially as the person has been dead for over two months and the temperature is in the high twenties. I wonder when he will be buried and what form the ceremony will take. With my limited knowledge, it's impossible to imagine. But I'm tired and soon fall into a fitful sleep.

Fresh from the shower, his sopping wet hair plastered to his head and dressed in clean clothes, PW presents himself in the clinic before eight o'clock, ready for work. He seems calm, even cheerful, as he greets me. I raise an eyebrow; it's one of the ways we communicate best. He points with his chin, up the road leading away from the settlement, in the opposite direction from Newman.

'All done, eh, Sis,' he says. 'Finished.'

'Buried?'

'Early.'

There'll be no more conversation between us about the funeral. Weeks later, Sandy and I would drive out along the road. We'd search for the burial ground but never find it.

The community nurse who works in Nullagine, in Nyamal country, rings to invite me to visit her. I'm pleased she's contacted me, but my Catholic conscience niggles.

'I don't think I should leave Jigalong,' I say.

'Nonsense!' she replies. 'The Director of Nursing thinks it's a good idea for us community nurses to see each other sometimes. We need to socialise, exchange ideas, encourage one another. Margaret and I often visit each other. Anyway, it's only a short drive, three hours at the most. Come for lunch. You can be back by five or six.'

I need little further persuasion. She tells me she's been working for the Health Department in this region for years, and if she thinks it's all right to leave Jigalong for something as frivolous as lunch, then I'll enjoy myself and see more of the Pilbara at the same time.

Pastoralists had settled in the Nullagine district in the early 1880s. When gold was discovered in 1888, the place became the centre of a minor gold rush. The present tiny town of Nullagine, with a population of around 300 people, is roughly 200 kilometres from Newman, north along the inland road to Marble Bar, also in Nyamal country, which is notorious for being the hottest town in Australia.

The community nurse had made her home in Nullagine many years before, and proudly took me on a sightseeing tour of an area so dry that year that water was rationed to strictly personal use even before Christmas. We drove to a tourist lookout and viewed land pockmarked with piles of dirt, and visited several of the tiny, abandoned mines where men had dug gold from the hard-baked ground with picks and shovels. We visited the gemstone factory and saw an extensive collection of semi-precious stones that had been gathered locally. We watched part of the polishing process, in which dirty, rough rocks were tumbled together in a bin for many hours until they emerged as smooth, lustrous objects of amazing colour and beauty. At the Conglomerate Hotel, the only one left in town, the nurse introduced me to the local customers while we ate fish and chips and crisp green salad. A congenial hostess, she was generous with her knowledge about community nursing and Aboriginal issues. I headed back to Jigalong a few hours later, as invigorated as if I'd had a week's holiday.

A fortnight after my visit, the nurse rang me.

'A young bloke died here last night,' she told me, distraught. 'There was nothing I could do to save him.'

I had no words to comfort her, and she left the town for good, later that day.

At Jigalong, the youth's mother and other relatives were frantic with grief and guilt, and the whole community was plunged into Sorry Business. Mournful wailing filled the air around the settlement. In the customary way, relatives punished themselves, inflicting lacerations when they smashed their own heads with billycans until their scalps were bruised and bleeding.

Sandy later told me that the mother of the boy who died was flogged as punishment. She said that when death occurred as the result of an accident, blame was apportioned according to the Law and the person or people thought to be responsible were punished, often severely. There was talk about nurses who were in real danger of being punished when a person in their care died, because they were perceived to have 'caused' the death.

Parents of young children were often too frightened to allow ill children to go to Perth for necessary treatment, in case the child died while he or she was in hospital. This was particularly heart-breaking when parents were told that surgery was necessary to save a child's life.

A toddler from Jigalong was diagnosed as having a heart defect that, unless treated by cardiac surgery, would lead to severe deterioration in his health and his eventual death. The surgeon explained to the parents that the operation carried a moderate risk, but without it the baby would certainly die before he could grow up. This placed the parents in an almost impossible position. If he died as the result of the surgery, they'd be held responsible for his death because they'd allowed the operation. If he died anyway, they would be blamed and punished also. Under considerable pressure from the health system, the couple finally agreed to the surgery in Perth and, to everyone's relief, the little boy made a full and uneventful recovery and returned to Jigalong.

23

I'm invited to go kangaroo shooting on a traditional hunting trip, augmented by four-wheel drive vehicles and guns. Now I've accepted, there's no time to think; they're leaving almost immediately. There's a buzz of excitement in the camp. About twenty fit young men, a few of the older men and some women and children are getting ready. I'm privileged to have been asked, but also very scared. I have no idea what I've agreed to or what I'll witness. The violence associated with guns repulses and frightens me, and the sight of a dozen rifles being loaded onto the backs of utilities and trucks, where the women and children are crammed together, does nothing to reassure me.

'It's best if you drive the ambulance,' Joannie decides.

'Do you expect there'll be an accident?' I ask warily.

'No. Just better if you drive, not sit in the back, eh. Too many women and kids.'

'That might be more fun,' I say. I know she's right, but I don't want to drive alone in the dark.

'Too rough. And on the way back the kangaroos will be in there, too,' she says in a no-nonsense voice.

'Are you coming?'

'No. Not this time. I'm getting too old.'

'You're twenty years younger than me!'

'Yo, but I'm too old,' she laughs. 'I've been a hundred times.'

'I'll come with you,' a woman standing nearby volunteers. She's slim and her voice and features are different from those of the Martu people. I notice immediately that she's wearing pretty sandals. 'I'm here for the school holidays, with my children. My husband works here,' she says, mentioning his name. 'You might know him?'

'Yes, I do know him. I'd love you to come with me,' I say gratefully.

We chat as we drive out of the settlement.

'I work as a teacher's aide in one of the kindergartens at home,' she tells me. 'But I'm studying to be a teacher, too. That's part time, because of the children.'

'You're not a Martu person?' I ask, seeking confirmation.

'No,' she replies. 'I live in a town, but I grew up in a community a bit like Jigalong, further south My husband's from there, too.'

The convoy drives slowly and soon turns off the familiar road to make our way along tracks I didn't know existed. I swerve repeatedly, avoiding the low scrubby acacia bushes on both sides. One or two scrape along the doors of the vehicle, and I hope they haven't scratched the paintwork. I follow the rest of the vehicles, shadowing the one immediately in front with total dedication. I grip the steering wheel tightly as we bump along, and my forehead feels taut from so much concentration. Suddenly, the tail lights I've been following disappear, we go over the top of an embankment of some sort and my stomach lurches sickeningly as we go down the other side.

'It's a creek,' the woman says. 'It's OK. We'll go along here a little way, then up again.'

The tail lights reappear, no more than thirty metres away. For a hundred metres we drive along the wide, uneven bed of the dry creek, and it takes all my strength to keep the wheels straight and the ambulance upright. It's a relief when we head up a gully and out onto flat land, and I notice that the banks of the creek are lined with small trees. I'm surprised how much bush there is in the area. I'd understood that there was little vegetation for miles around.

Ahead in the distance spotlights weave across the flat ground. Occasionally, a light beams to the top of a solitary tree. One light sweeps backwards and forwards across the sky. It reminds me forcibly of a childhood terror of wartime searchlights, a fear induced by boy cousins older than me who assured me solemnly that, if you saw a light during a blackout in Perth, you'd be shot.

'The men are looking for kangaroos, now,' the woman says. 'They're searching for any sign. This is good country.'

'It's eerie here in the dark, with so many people with loaded guns,' I say. 'I've never been shooting before.'

The words don't come close to expressing my nervousness. I don't tell her that my palms are sticky with sweat on the steering wheel.

'You're all right,' she reassures me. 'Nothing can happen to us this far away.'

'I'm glad you're with me,' I say. 'I don't know how I'd have managed by myself.'

'I'd rather be with you than on the back of one of those trucks,' she laughs.

'Why have you decided to be a teacher?' I ask when we are on the flat, and I've regained easy control of the vehicle. 'That must be hard, with four children, and working too.'

'Yes, it's hard,' she agrees. 'But they're part of the reason. I want to give them a better life than I had. My husband and I both do.'

'Most Aboriginal people have a harder life than I can imagine,' I comment. 'And the difficulties have become much clearer to me since I've been at Jigalong.'

'Yes. It's the same old story, really. We lived on a reserve outside a town. My father sold me many times, to white men, when I was a kid.' She says it in a matter-of-fact voice, without anger, without bitterness.

'That's terrible,' I say, barely comprehending what her life must have been like.

'It was. The price they paid for my body was a flagon of sherry.'

'Yet you're so calm.' I'm in awe of this woman who has been comforting me in my childish fear.

'In some ways I've been very lucky,' she continues. 'I've got a good life now. My husband never hits me. And we look after the children together. We're bringing them up properly.'

'You deserve all the good things you can get.'

'And, when I finish my degree, it will be even better. Then I can help my people the way my husband does already. There are still young girls and women, too, in many of the communities, abused the way I was. Not just in communities, either. In the towns and on the reserves on the fringes of the towns. And many women are beaten when their men are drunk.'

'Yes, I've seen some of them, already.'

We've driven about thirty kilometres since we left the settlement, but I've been so concerned with following and not getting lost or bogged in the soft dirt at the sides of the track that it seems much further. Eventually the convoy stops. By the time I've drawn up to the other vehicles and turned off the engine, the men who'd been leading have already shot four kangaroos. I'm glad it's over and at the same time, in a perverse twist, disappointed I've missed the shooting.

'These fellows shoot for sport, not for food,' my companion remarks, 'although they'll have a feed as well.'

The men stand around to admire their booty lying dead and twitching at their feet. The men look ferocious in the spotlights that distort their features and throw giant shadows behind them. They drag the bleeding carcasses to the vehicles, to a chorus of jubilant shouts and admiring squeals and calls from the women and children.

Men extract joeys from the pouches of two kangaroos and hand them to some adolescent girls who are sitting in the tray of a truck. The girls seize the scrawny, hairless bodies and exclaim and coo over them tenderly, their minds apparently detached from the slaughtered bodies of the mother kangaroos. The joeys will be passed from hand to hand and stroked and cuddled until the girls are bored, and later they'll be eaten, like the adult kangaroos.

The men throw the carcasses carelessly onto the utes and trucks, and the guns on top of them. The women and children climb back in and arrange themselves in the diminished area around the bodies, balancing dangerously with some of the children sitting on each other's knees. The whole proceedings are over in less than fifteen minutes and we drive back to the settlement along a different route. It's quicker than the way out, and we bump along at a reasonable pace. I'm even more nervous now, because there's the possibility I won't be able to keep up and I might get lost.

Back in Jigalong the slaughtered animals are gutted, skinned and dismembered outside the store, then thrown onto waiting campfires. It happens quickly and I work hard to disguise my disgust at the sight of torn, bloodied flesh. There's a stench of burning fur and meat in the air and I escape quickly to my flat before someone can offer me any.

24

'You'd better stay here this morning,' Joannie says one day soon after the kangaroo shoot. 'There's big trouble with one of the women.'

There's no point in asking questions, not even when she tells me she's going out.

There's a tight knot of women up the road, past the school and the store. I'm curious but not brave enough to satisfy my curiosity by leaving the clinic after Joannie's warning. I can hear a bloodcurdling roar, like an uncontrolled mob of barrackers at a football match. The commotion subsides and there's a lull for a few seconds before a single voice shouts what sounds like a command.

Immediately there's another sound, far more spinechilling than the shouting. Thwack … thwack … thwack … thwack. This is the 'big trouble' Joannie warned me about. The noise enters my ears and reverberates in my head. I want to run away, but I'm transfixed at the window. I can't comprehend what it must be like to be the victim, set upon by so many other women. Does she cower on the ground, cover her head and her ears with her arms, or does she stand still and straight and accept the beating courageously? What was her crime? What does it mean to be one of the women who can hit another so viciously?

Suddenly the beating is over and the mob disperses. The women walk sedately, some arm in arm, back to their own camps. I recognise many of them, usually kind, gentle women who bring their children and their old mothers and aunts to the clinic. I wait for someone to bring the victim to the clinic, but nothing happens. Perhaps, although it seems impossible, she's not badly injured.

After lunch when there's no one around I walk along the road past the store to the place where the beating was carried out. The area is unmistakable; scuffling feet have disturbed the dust in a large circle and there are marks where the woman has been dragged away.

Someone has left behind a club-like object. Mesmerised, I pick it up and take it back to the clinic. It's a piece of wandoo about the thickness of a child's arm, beautifully crafted and balanced like a baseball bat, with a knob at one end that fits comfortably into the palm of my hand. The surface has been rubbed smooth and oiled until it's shiny. Delicate marks have been carved into the wood along the handle, no doubt telling a story to those who know how to read it.

'It's a woman's hitting stick,' Joannie confirms when I show it to her. 'It's mostly for killing small animals.'

We don't discuss the flogging but I'm sure she guesses where I picked up the hitting stick.

PW puts his head around the door. He's out of breath.

'There's big punishment going on,' he says. 'It's a floggen. By the store.'

'What —' I begin, but he cuts me off.

'Be ready,' he warns. 'We'll bring 'im 'ere. After.'

'Ready? For what?'

But PW runs off and I'm left full of dread, imagining what might be happening while I stand there and worry about how I can prepare myself and the clinic to receive what could be a broken and bloody body.

I find him after lunch, slumped on the rough concrete at the edge of the path, half on, half off the verandah outside the clinic. There's a thin trickle of blood from his nose and one of his eyes is swollen shut. Blood pools slowly on the ground under his dreadlocked hair, which is wet and sticky-looking. His right leg has buckled underneath him, the bone probably broken. He looks as if he's been dumped from a vehicle by someone in a hurry to get away.

'Hi there,' I say, squatting beside him, my mouth close to his ear. 'What happened?'

He opens the undamaged eye, tries to move his head, moans and then mumbles something unintelligible. I'm not sure if he's speaking in his own language or in English. Perhaps it's neither.

'It's OK,' I say. 'You'll be OK.'

It comes automatically, a nurse's platitude meant to reassure him, although there's no guarantee he will be all right and, despite my professionally calm voice, inside I'm panicking.

He slumps back and I see he's only a youngster, no more than sixteen or seventeen years old. I look around, not really expecting to see anyone, but hoping I'm wrong. Most days by this time a group of people would have gathered on the verandah, waiting to see me or hoping to rest in the clinic, away from the heat of the afternoon sun. But there's no one. If this boy has been punished according to customary law, I understand it will be wrong for anyone to help me.

The first time no one came when I needed help, I was puzzled. I'd grown accustomed to working in front of an audience — the concerned, the curious and the bored almost always appeared at the doorway with a patient who was seriously ill or injured. Occasionally, though, everyone hid away, not wanting to be part of the spectacle, perhaps afraid of being implicated in something I didn't understand.

'Where were you when I needed help? And where was everyone else?' I had asked PW and Joannie, aggrieved.

They answered with careful little shrugs, their eyes averted. Clearly they thought it was none of my business, and I was ashamed of my outburst.

Now I'm all alone and lonely. I'm scared the boy's going to die. I take a few deep breaths to steady myself while I think about my predicament. The teachers are away for the school holidays and I had watched enviously last night when the other white residents headed off together. They packed swags and eskys full of ice and food into the back of four-wheel drive vehicles. They've gone to look for a waterhole we've been talking about for weeks, and they plan to camp out until Monday night. I promise myself I'll find a way to go with them the next time they celebrate a long weekend.

The only person who can help is the new mechanic, if he hasn't gone into town or off exploring. He's just arrived in the settlement and I've only met him briefly, earlier in the week, but we haven't spoken except to say hello. Like nurses, mechanics come and go with regularity; the work is hard and the heat and dust oppressive. He lives at the other end of the settlement. I'll have to find a way to get a message to him, asking him to come to the clinic. But that's a problem I can leave until later.

I weigh up the chances of causing more injury by leaving the boy where he is. The sun is relentless and there will be no shade from the overhang of the verandah until much later in the afternoon. The concrete will burn him if I leave him where he is, and I'll be sunburned if I'm out there too long. I could make a temporary shelter, but that will take time and we don't have that luxury. I have no choice, I decide. I must find a way to get him under cover without inflicting further harm.

'I'm going inside to get a few things,' I tell him. 'I'll be back soon.'

He doesn't answer. Not even a flicker of an eyelid tells me he's heard.

I grab the first-aid box and a thin mattress and carry them outside. I fossick in the box until I find what I need. To staunch the bleeding, I put a pressure pad on the wound on his scalp and bandage it in place. His head is heavy and rolls from side to side while I work and I steady it against my body. Then I cut off the leg of his jeans and discover it is not his femur that is broken, but the smaller bones below the knee. I splint his leg as well as I can, using the bright blue inflatable splints from the first-aid box and a couple of triangular bandages. It's a crude job but it keeps the broken bones stable and by the time I've finished the boy has stopped moaning.

'How does that feel?' I ask. 'Better?'

I don't expect an answer, so I'm surprised when he opens his good eye again and looks at me for a few seconds.

'Now I'm going to put you on this mattress and take you inside,' I tell him. When I say it like that, it sounds easy. 'If you lie still, it won't take very long. You'll be more comfortable then.'

It takes ages to pull him onto the mattress, but it's easier than trying to use the stretcher. By slow degrees, resting often, I haul the boy into the treatment room on the mattress. I'm panting and my arms and back ache from the exertion by the time I abandon the task and leave him in the middle of the green linoleum. I reassess his injuries and find they are even worse than I first thought. I apply more pressure pads to the deepest wounds, and check his pulse and blood pressure before I phone the RFDS.

'It'll take us a couple of hours to get a plane in the air,' the operator says. 'The doc's not around right now, either.'

'Oh,' I say, consciously keeping my voice steady to disguise my panic. 'When will he be back?'

'He's not far away.' There's a pause and I imagine she flicks through a diary to check the medical officer's schedule.

'I think he's taken his little boy fishing.'

'Fishing!'

'It's a long weekend,' she says reasonably. 'Just because we are working ...' Her voice trails off. 'We'll be there soon,' she continues briskly. 'I shouldn't have told you where he was. Anyway, he'll be back before I round up the pilot. You can always ring one of the city hospitals if you're worried.'

'Yeah, thanks,' I say before I hang up. At this rate I can't expect relief before dark.

I consult with a registrar from one of the teaching hospitals in the city thousands of kilometres away. She sounds as if she hasn't any idea where I am, or the conditions I'm working in, but I follow her directions anyway, to the best of my ability. I give my patient an injection to ease the pain, and suture some of the lacerations. I clean and dress smaller wounds and put ice packs on the worst bruises. All the time, I'm monitoring and recording his vital signs — blood pressure, pulse, breathing rate, state of consciousness.

Some children come into the clinic compound. They're doing noisy kid-things and I don't have time to watch.

'Hello,' I call from the door. 'Will you take a note to the mechanic, please?'

One of the older girls saunters over to the verandah.

'We're not s'posed to be 'ere,' she says. 'But I will.'

'Thanks,' I say. 'I won't be long.'

I'm reluctant to let her out of my sight in case she wanders off or changes her mind, so I take a scrap of paper and a biro from my pocket and quickly scribble a note.

There's a jar of jellybeans on the bench near the door and I grab a handful and thrust them with the note into the child's hands.

'It's important,' I say. 'Can you give it to him quickly, please? Do you know where he lives?'

She nods briefly and ambles off in the direction of the other children, calling out to them as she goes. I hope she won't be distracted on the way, and that the mechanic will be home. Most of all, I hope she doesn't encounter an adult who will prevent her from helping the man on my floor.

'Thank God you've come,' I greet the young man when he appears at the door half an hour later. 'I wasn't sure you'd get the message.'

'Yup,' he says. 'I came straight away.' He notices the boy on the floor and quickly averts his eyes. 'Jesus! Will he be all right?'

'Hope so. I'm working on it, and the RFDS is on its way. Can you light the airstrip before sunset?'

'Dunno,' he says cheerfully. 'But I can have a go. It'll be my first time. There's a page of instructions back at the workshop. Should be able to follow them.'

'Great,' I say. 'Thanks. And when the plane comes, will you give the doctor a lift back here, please?'

It's dusk before I hear the drone of the plane. Suddenly the RFDS medical officer and nurse seem like my best friends. I let myself relax and immediately feel my energy dissipate. The wait has felt interminable, and when they push open the door, I'm bending over the boy and barely greet them. They're unconcerned — exhausted nurses are no novelty to them.

When the doctor has stabilised the boy ready for the flight, the three of us lift him onto the stretcher and then into the ambulance. The doctor climbs into the back, his left hand holding a flask of saline high above the intravenous line which disappears into the arm of the boy who is lying inert under the sheet on the stretcher. The flight nurse hoists herself up onto the passenger seat, fastens her seat belt, and leans back. I'm the last one in and I position myself behind the wheel and drive slowly to the edge of the settlement and onto the track.

We pass the football oval with its gravel surface and crooked goalposts, and lurch deep into the creek bed where it loops back on itself. After the rains it will contain a surging torrent that will flood the road and cut off access to the plane. The headlights pick out a thin kangaroo bounding along three or four metres ahead of the vehicle. The animal veers off to the left and I drive on grimly, trying to anticipate and correct the bumps and jolts along the way.

Battered vehicles in a variety of shapes and sizes line the far side of the four-strand cattle fence that marks the perimeter of the airstrip at the southern fringe of the settlement. The smell of kerosene hangs in the air from the lamps that line both sides of the bush runway, lighting a path towards the horizon. Light from the open door of the plane on the runway spills onto the crowd that has gathered since news of an evacuation spread around the community with the arrival of the plane.

We reach the fence and I nose the ambulance towards the gate. Someone runs over to open the rickety post-and-wire construction. I drive through with a wave of thanks. The headlights on high beam pick out the crowd that is waiting for us.

The pilot leans against one of the rough saplings that hold up the bark-covered roof of a primitive shelter erected on this desolate strip. He's talking to the mechanic and takes no notice of the crowd at the edge of the darkness — men wearing black football shorts and jeans, some torn; women, their hair moving in the hot night breeze, with fretting babies in their arms; children chasing each other, yelling, fighting. A couple of dingo-cross dogs wander in and out between skinny legs, around bare feet and filthy thongs made in Taiwan.

The pilot looks at his watch and glances towards the horizon. The lights have been burning since sunset, hours ago, and he will know all too well from hundreds of other landings and take-offs the delay the plane and its passengers will face if the lamps have to be refilled and relit.

I reverse the ambulance towards the plane and turn off the ignition. The pilot waves as we pull up, and then looks at his watch one more time, probably estimating how long it will take before they can be airborne. He flicks open the door of the ambulance and he and the doctor lift the stretcher smoothly out onto the ground. A man in a red headband steps forward from the crowd and supervises them closely. The stretcher is raised on its frame and wheeled to the plane, where it is placed carefully inside. Through the open door of the tiny aircraft I see the flight nurse and doctor busy with the patient. They strap him in, hang the saline flask on the hook above his head and check his pulse and blood pressure.

With a quick wave and a shouted 'Bye!' the flight nurse closes the door. Dust and gravel pepper the faces of the watchers as the plane accelerates down the runway into the wind. Soon the vehicles along the fence move off, back towards the camps. Three young women separate themselves from the remaining crowd.

'Give us a ride back, Sis?' one of them asks shyly.

'Hop in,' I say, knowing they'll expect to be delivered to their doors.

I'm preoccupied, thinking about the mess I've left behind — the pile of bloodstained towels and sheets to be washed and hung on the line in the dark; the mattress on the floor; and the scissors and forceps and dishes I threw in the sink, not even rinsed. I'll clean up quickly when I get back, I tell myself, and leave everything ready for tomorrow's dramas. Suddenly I remember how exhausted and lonely, hungry and thirsty, I am.

'Race you down the runway,' calls the mechanic, pulling up next to me. 'If you give me a hand to put out the lights we can have a coffee together.'

Coffee and company!

I wave as I put the ambulance into gear, my foot on the accelerator, and speed away. It's a smooth ride, a graded surface, but the fence won't keep stray kangaroos off it. My passengers shriek in the seat behind me. The vehicles reach the farthest lights together. We pause. I opt for the right-side row. I stop, jump out and snuff the first light, climb back in, and drive to the next, counting down. There are fifteen more in the long line in front of us.

'Would one of you put out the next light, please?' I ask the women as I stop for the second time. 'I thought we could take it in turns.'

There's a long pause.

'Oh, no, Sis!' they chorus, shocked. '*Ladies* don't put out the lights.'

25

Margaret slips back into the settlement quietly, six weeks after she left. When I go outside one Monday morning her ute is in the driveway, and in the air there's a whiff of bread toasting.

'How was the conference?' I ask when she walks into the clinic half an hour later.

'Not bad, thanks. Yes, pretty good, really. How's it been here?'

'Not bad, thanks.'

'Heard in Hedland that you've done OK without me.'

'Thanks. Interesting work,' I say.

The workload halved. We shared the weekend and after hours' drudgery, although my colleague did not seem to think of it like that. I turned my attention to the preventative work I'd thought I'd been employed to do, screening children in the school for sight and hearing defects and developmental delays. I began to plan and deliver health education programs. Margaret worked to catch up with the mothers-and-babies program that I'd neglected while she was away. She was again the nurse-in-charge and I was relieved and thankful to have her back. For the most part, I was happy to do as I was told.

Politicians from both sides of government and heads of departments invite themselves to Jigalong to discuss the needs and wants of the community. They'll bring other bureaucrats with them, as well as representatives of non-government welfare agencies who have also been invited.

A social worker and her boss, an older man, arrive at sunset from Newman in a vehicle with their department's logo barely visible under the dust. They pull up at our gate and I go outside to greet them; I've agreed the woman can billet with me for a night or two. I haven't had any outside visitors since I've been here and the thought of company pleases me.

'Come in and make yourself at home,' I say. 'You can put your gear on my sitting room floor. Sorry I don't have a spare bed.'

'A swag is more fun,' she laughs. 'And mine is very comfortable.'

She's just a girl, I think, as I watch her unload her swag and an overnight bag from the vehicle. She hefts the tight bundle of bedclothes in their canvas cover into my flat. A flurry of dust rises and settles when she drops it on the floor. With her knees flexed, she bends and unbuckles the leather straps that hold the swag together. A practised push from her foot unrolls it on the floor. Next, she brings in an icebox and dumps it on the kitchen bench.

'I brought fresh fruit and my favourite cheeses and some salad things,' she says shyly. 'I heard you don't often get to town, so I thought you might like them.'

She unpacks the provisions and stows them in the refrigerator. Over a meal, she tells me she came to the Pilbara almost straight from university.

'It was to have been my big adventure,' she says wryly. 'I'd planned it for a couple of years and thought I was lucky to get this job. But I hate the heat. And I miss my family,' she confides. 'Sometimes I can't remember why I came. Everything's so different. It's like a foreign country, isn't it? I feel as if I can't talk to people who've never been here because they don't understand. And people who live up here permanently are so comfortable they're almost smug.'

In the morning, we sit on the verandah with toast and coffee on the table between us and watch a stream of bureaucrats inundate the settlement. Some come from Port Hedland in tiny planes that bump along the runway before they stop by the bush shelter on the airstrip. Men and women get out, clean and crisp in ironed shorts and shirts. They are collected from the airstrip by staff from the community office. Others drive themselves, two and three to a vehicle, from Newman. We watch clouds of dust on the horizon come closer then disappear, as each conveyance dips into the dry creek before it materialises at the gates of the settlement.

The new arrivals wave and call to each other, noisily asserting their right to be at Jigalong. They generate an air of bravado like nervous tourists on the first day of an adventure trek when no one can predict what will happen next, and everyone hopes they'll soon stop feeling incongruous. They set off purposefully to the office to be given directions and keys to the places where they'll sleep when the business of the day is over, and to put their luggage inside, making space for themselves.

Accommodation is tight, but somehow beds have been found for everyone. Most visitors claim the units that, in spite of the substandard housing and overcrowding in the settlement, have been permanently set aside for the exclusive, occasional use of their agencies. There's been an unusual flurry of activity as the settlement prepared to receive guests. Neglected buildings have been swept and mopped and dusted, although red dust still sticks in streaks to furniture and floors.

Yesterday, Margaret and I cleaned the empty three-bedroom house at the back of the health compound where senior doctors and nurses and bureaucrats from the Health Department will eat and sleep. In the past, it's been used by nurses who bravely brought families with them when they came to work here.

Everywhere, bedding has been aired, sheets and towels found, washed and dried in the sun. Air-conditioning units are turned on, jugs of water placed in refrigerators and ice trays in freezers.

A three-sided asbestos shed has been set up for the meeting. The structure provides shade but holds the heat. Originally built as a shearing shed, it has been used for many things over the years. It bears the scars of much misuse, too, with jagged holes big enough to walk through. Some of the graffiti is obscene. The floor is so dirty that no amount of sweeping or hosing would clean it. The easterly wind from the desert blows in through the open side, propelling sand in front of it, stinging our eyes and prickling our skin.

My house guest perches on the edge of a white plastic chair, fanning herself with a dog-eared government-issue writing pad. She's scribbled on several of the pages, doodled on several more. But she's given up trying to take notes, and waits miserably for the day to end. Her khaki tailored shorts and once-white linen shirt cling, crumpled and damp, to her body. Blonde tendrils have escaped from her drawn-back hair and curl around her flushed face. Her shoulders droop. From time to time, she rummages in the big leather handbag at her feet, pulls out crumpled tissues and dabs at her forehead and her top lip. This does not look like a pleasant experience for her. I imagine she'll be glad to be back in Newman after her foray this far into the desert.

The politicians and other speakers are arranged along one side of a table at the front. The leaders of the Jigalong Community Incorporated and less important government workers sit stiffly on chairs in rows on each side, facing the speakers' table and overlooking the groups scattered around on the dirty cement. Martu women sit together, cross-legged, drinking thirstily from Coca-Cola cans and smoking cigarettes. They talk among themselves in muffled voices, not always understanding what's being said, but not wanting to disrupt the speakers. Toddlers in T-shirts and bare bottoms stagger between the women. They're intent on keeping their balance and oblivious to the importance of the meeting. Hands reach out to steady them, touch them, stroke them. The children clutch at their mothers' clothing. Fat babies suck at the breasts they knead and pound with tiny fists. They wriggle their toes with pleasure, movement that reminds me of the wagging tails of suckling lambs. Dogs stretch out on the ground, eyes half closed against the sun and wind and sand. Ears twitch.

Young men lean against the bush posts at the open side of the shed. They nudge each other, flick cigarettes into the sand outside and whisper. Old men clump together off to the side, sometimes muttering to themselves and each other. The language of government officials isn't their language, even though some strain to make sense of what they hear. They are resigned, anyway. Nothing will change. A couple of them doze off, heads nod.

'We want to hear your opinion,' pontificates one of the politicians, enunciating each word slowly. 'That is why we have come to your community. We want to find out what your ideas are so we can do our best for you.'

'Nothing new,' Margaret whispers. 'The Martu people have heard this before. We all have.'

'But I thought the politicians and everyone want to make a difference,' I whisper back.

'They've got good intentions,' she says, shifting her weight on the ground. 'But bush meetings haven't changed anything in the past, and this one won't make much difference, either. It's not as if these bureaucrats have any power. Or that they'll take notice of what the Martu tell them.'

An hour into the meeting, when we pause for morning tea, the new senior medical officer for the Pilbara makes a beeline to where Margaret and I have been sitting on the ground with the other women.

'You need to fix the air-conditioning in that house where I'm staying — the one behind the clinic,' the man demands. It's the first thing he's said to either of us since he arrived. 'And there's no water for a shower. You need to get that fixed, too.'

'Sorry,' Margaret says meekly. 'The water and electricity went off this morning. Perhaps the generator's broken.' She smiles sweetly at him. 'It happens, out here in the desert. We don't have mains power or scheme water.'

A Martu woman who has been listening to this conversation smiles gently as our eyes meet. She raises one shoulder. Ever so slightly.

26

My father, Keith Stone, writes letters full of moving stories about a recent holiday with my sister in Bangkok. Like me, he'd never had much desire to travel before Elizabeth went to Thailand. Now he's seeking new experiences, he says, and wishes he was ten years younger. He suggests his next holiday could be with me, at Jigalong. I'm pleased but cautious. He's an old man. Should he need health services, Jigalong is a long way from the health care services available in the towns and cities.

'A holiday in Jigalong would be like nothing you've experienced,' I tell him when he rings. 'There's none of the spectacle of Thailand. It's very different.'

'I'm sure that's an understatement, dear.'

'My flat's so small it would fit comfortably into the sitting room in Elizabeth's apartment. And it's brown. There's no maid to help me look after you, like there was in Bangkok,' I joke. 'And my cooking's deteriorated unbelievably.'

'Perhaps I could cook for you, sometimes, then,' he retorts.

'That'd be nice. What you'd cook would depend on what was in the store, or what I'd remembered to order from Newman. But I'd love you to come.'

I try to tell him about the country: its dry redness that glows purple at dawn and orange at sunset and all shades of red in between. I talk about the mysteries of the robust, richly evolving culture around me, with its ancient foundations, the imposed traumas of white settlement and the overlay of modern Australian culture, some of which the Martu people have adopted with enthusiasm. It's difficult to describe the way the culture has evolved and continues to evolve, creating values and beliefs that are new and different from anything that has gone before — a palimpsest, continually rewritten — while maintaining continuity with the past.

'There's not much to do here, unless you are working,' I say. 'But if you come, you're welcome to wander between the flat and the clinic. They're both air-conditioned. You can watch me at work. Everyone else does.'

'I can amuse myself. You needn't worry. I'll bring a book or two.'

Margaret warms to the idea of a visitor. 'I'll work both weekends,' she volunteers generously. 'I'm fresh after my holiday. Then you can spend more time with your dad.'

There was a mile of red tape to be unravelled before an outsider could visit the settlement. First, I had to obtain permission from the Health Department because Dad would be staying with me in accommodation they provided, even though I paid the rent. Next, I needed written permission from the Commonwealth Department of Aboriginal Affairs, which claimed responsibility for Aboriginal reserves.

Finally, I asked Jigalong Community Incorporated, the body responsible for the running of the settlement. The request for a visit by the father of the nurse had to be discussed and deliberated but, in the end, I had a sheaf of papers in a file, and permission from everyone in authority.

In some Aboriginal settlements in other parts of Australia, people produce art, craft and artefacts. They enjoy a growing tourism industry which brings the dollars into their communities. Jigalong was no tourist destination. On the contrary, a deliberate decision had been made in an attempt to limit further undermining of traditional culture and customary law, and tourism was actively discouraged. Intending visitors applied in writing for permission to enter the settlement and were accepted only if they could prove adequate grounds for being there. Rare, accidental travellers — those who had, perhaps, lost their way in the desert — would find no accessible accommodation, not even a camping area. The music they heard would more likely be country and western than didgeridoo; no one would dance a corroboree for them, nor would they find anyone making or selling art or craft. The only fuel was diesoline; there was no petrol. This, also, was a deliberate decision, one that made it difficult for bored children and young people to sniff petrol. It had the added effect of discouraging visitors in petrol-fuelled vehicles.

'My dad's coming to stay with me soon,' I tell a group of young women. 'I'm looking forward to it.'

They observe me gravely.

'Your dad must be very old,' one of them says with some wonder.

'Yes, he's not a young man,' I reply.

'He must be ancient.' She pauses, thinking. 'Because *you* are so old,' she adds.

'I don't feel old,' I say, amused because I don't think I'm old. But age is no laughing matter in a community where men and women over forty are called 'the old grannies' and life expectancy is around fifty years.

The sky is brilliant in the setting sun and the heat of the day still sears the air, living up to the promise I'd made my father. He holds the rail tightly as he comes down the gangway from the plane in Newman, and appears more stooped and frail than when I last saw him, a few months ago. But the hug he gives me on the tarmac is as comforting and reaffirming as ever and his voice is as strong as it always was.

The flat in Newman, booked for our overnight stopover, has the carefree ambiance of a holiday house, one well used and enjoyed. There are mementoes and evidence of other people's recent occupation: a couple of Mills & Boon novels, their unmistakable pink-printed covers slightly dog-eared; a science fiction novel; a *West Australian* newspaper from yesterday; and a bunch of wildflowers left to dry on a window sill. The air-conditioning unit works efficiently, if noisily, and the place is passably clean and wonderfully comfortable for our short stay.

From there we set off to explore, at least superficially, some of the spectacular gorges in the Karijini National Park, between Newman and the coast. The tourist brochures that litter the back seat of our luxurious hired car tell us that the best way to experience the park is to walk, climb and swim, all impossible given Dad's frailty. But it's exhilarating to stand at the top of a gorge — a cleft in rocks that frames waterfalls and still, green pools over a hundred metres below where we stand.

'The earth has been torn apart,' Dad reflects. 'It's hard to comprehend the forces of nature that could do that.'

'One day, I plan to hike and climb here. And sleep in a swag under the stars,' I say. 'I'd like to climb down and inch along the ledges and squeeze through the caves. But I'd want someone with me who could rescue me if I fell.'

'Well, I wouldn't be much good at that,' he laughs. 'But it's hard to remember I'll be eighty this month.'

Wittenoom, in Banjima country, is the site of one of Australia's largest industrial disasters. It nestles at the edge of the beautiful Wittenoom Gorge on the northern boundary of the park. It is almost a ghost town. Buildings are boarded up, houses deserted and services have been withdrawn. Most residents left as a result of persistent government warnings that the legacy of asbestos mining renders the town lethal. Inhalation of the sharp, very fine blue fibres of asbestos, used for insulation and building, has slowly killed over 1000 people through deadly diseases such as asbestosis, lung cancer and mesothelioma. The number of deaths is still rising.

Tailings from the mine are spread around the town; they had once been used for paths in gardens and street verges, and as a surface for the yards of the two schools and the racecourse. Some of the asbestos has been covered over, but this does not prevent the risk of inhalation. The town and the area surrounding it are beautiful, but there's an air of desolation. Scrupulously, we follow instructions from signs that warn us to keep the car windows up in windy weather and not to walk in some areas. I'm glad I've seen the place, but am relieved to drive away.

Dad invites some old women, visitors to the settlement from an outstation, to afternoon tea on the verandah. Between them they speak about twenty words of English. I've always considered Dad a cultured man. He grew up in a wealthy, conservative family where restrained British good manners were an imperative. He observes calmly as the women carefully spoon quantities of sugar into their cups of tea, and dunk their biscuits until they fall apart and float in the syrup. He watches impassively as they transfer the soggy remnants to their mouths with their fingers and drink noisily from their saucers.

When they've finished eating and drinking, one of the women produces a crumpled plastic bag and takes out several tiny coolamons, basin-like containers for carrying seeds or water, constructed from bark and decorated with patterns burned into the sides. The women set the coolamons proudly on the table in puddles of milk and sugar.

'How much?' asks my dad, recently returned from the markets of Bangkok where he's learned to barter.

'Hundred dollar.'

'A hundred dollars?'

'Hundred dollar,' they chorus, laughing.

Dad looks at me for support, hoping, perhaps, for some guidance. I smile and shrug. This is the first time I've seen art or craft for sale at Jigalong.

'Maybe five dollars?' he counters, but they don't understand his words or intent and they laugh together as if they share an enormous joke. At the end of the transaction, Dad takes his wallet from his back pocket and gravely hands each of the women a ten-dollar note. In return, they coquettishly hand over their craft objects.

A local man and the project officer, whose wife went with me on the kangaroo shoot, invite Dad and me on a sightseeing trip out of Jigalong.

'It'll be a great experience,' Margaret says enthusiastically. 'You'll have a good time.'

When the men come to the flat to collect us early the next morning, there are ten noisy children intent on exploiting a school-free day crammed into the back of a pick-up truck. After a drive of about twenty kilometres, the project officer stops the vehicle beside a sizeable waterhole which is contained by craggy rocks and surrounded by casuarina trees and mulga.

I've prepared a picnic — chicken and sausages, bread and butter, salad, a chocolate cake and the ubiquitous apples, all packed in an esky. I planned the picnic for a leisurely lunch but, as soon as the vehicle stops at the edge of the waterhole, the bigger boys hoist the esky over the tailboard. They tear the lid off before it hits the ground. The food is distributed and eaten within minutes. The children run whooping and shouting towards the pool, where they wade and swim and splash on the edges. We adults follow sedately.

The project officer points out carvings, high above us on some of the rocks.

'There are more markings on rocks lower down, but you won't be able to get close enough to look at them,' he tells us. 'It's too steep.'

'All them carvings tell stories,' the other man adds. 'Stories about how things happened long, long time ago.'

The men swim across the waterhole to the far side, where they stand chatting in waist-deep water, while the children play on the edge close to us. Dad settles himself in sparse shade with a wet handkerchief to wipe his face and a litre of drinking water at his side. I sit on a rock near him with my feet in the water, watching the children and men. I'd been too shy to ask if it would be all right for me to swim, too, but when the heat becomes unbearable and sweat is pouring down my face and between my breasts and shoulderblades I slide carefully over the side of the rock. If I keep to the edge of the pool where it is knee-deep, where the children are, I tell myself, it will be OK. The water is so wonderfully cool it almost takes my breath away as I lower myself fully clothed into it.

'We were watching you,' the project officer says when we're ready to go home. 'We thought you'd swim across.'

'No. I wasn't sure if it was all right,' I reply. 'I thought it was a special place.'

'I should have said something. I didn't think. The kids already know they mustn't swim too far out.'

'I thought it best not to swim at all so I watched the kids, and did what they did, until I was cool.'

'That's right. This isn't a place for women to swim, especially not a white woman. But you did well. You stayed by the rocks on the edge, the place for women and little kids.'

★　　★　　★

The project officer shares our evening meal a day or two later. 'Dinner' is a concept I've almost forgotten, and seem much too pretentious. I roast a chicken and bake vegetables with dried rosemary, a passable substitute for the sprigs of fresh herbs that grow outside my kitchen door at home. I set the table carefully, using the new cloth Dad has brought me as a gift, in response to my plea for something in gentle pastels that would be a relief from the vibrant colours of the desert. The nurses' flats were not designed for entertaining, and the three of us crowd around the small table.

The project officer is employed by the Jigalong Council. He shares their values and belief system and has versatile, practical skills and a different kind of wisdom to impart to the Martu men, especially the younger ones. He talks about many fascinating topics that I suspect would never have been raised in my company if my father hadn't been there.

Twelve days after he arrived, I take Dad to the plane in Newman to return to Perth to celebrate his eightieth birthday at a party to be held in his honour the following weekend. I am sad to miss the celebration of this important milestone, and even sadder to see him leave. He promises to give everyone my love and to send me photos and birthday cake. He is pleased when Margaret asks him to escort a fifteen-year-old boy who needs surgery in Perth. I make no attempt to hide my tears when I say goodbye.

Thank you, my dear, for such a wonderful break, Dad wrote a few days later. *The trip to the Hamersley Gorges was out of this world. I don't often seriously express regrets about growing older, but now I really wish I were ten years younger. I would buy a four-wheel drive and spend maybe twelve months exploring the north-west. You know, Port Hedland, Derby, Broome, the Ord River area. Anywhere.*

The Gorges, however, were not the only delights. In the short time I was there, I developed quite a feeling for Jigalong — flat, dusty sometimes, sprawling, sort of unplanned; and the weather was kind to me. Your hospitality exactly fitted my mood. I enjoyed drinking coffee and watching the bustle in the clinic, and the RFDS evacuation was an experience I would not have missed. Dinner on Tuesday with (the project officer) *was very enlightening. I only wish I'd found out more about his childhood, but I'm a bit slow to ask about that sort of thing.*

Elizabeth and I put the young man I accompanied on the plane into a taxi at the airport, with a kind woman taxi driver who agreed to deliver him to the door of the hostel that is attached to the hospital in Perth.

Thank you again for a wonderful holiday.

Love, KS

P.S. I have written to the Chair of the Council to thank him for letting me visit.

27

Minor differences surfaced between Margaret and me, mostly about inconsequential issues and disparities in our nursing styles. Her manner was relaxed, unfazed; she'd worked in the outback for years and had a depth of experience to draw from, as well as a wealth of hands-on knowledge and appreciation of Aboriginal people.

I had no such familiarity. Instead, my previous experience included work as the quality assurance officer in a major teaching hospital. I had a passion for policy and procedures, combined with fastidiousness about cleaning as I went, documenting what I'd done and knowing who was accountable for what. My predilection for dotting 'i's and crossing 't's must have irritated her, just as I deplored her more casual approach to the work we shared. Because there was nowhere else to go, no one to appeal to, we managed to paper over most of the difficulties and co-exist comfortably, but sometimes I fumed, and possibly Margaret did, too.

Late one Sunday night PW brings three older men to the clinic. They've been in a fight. One has a gash on his head and another a deep wound in his calf muscle. They all have multiple lacerations. The larger wounds bleed profusely. Only sutures will stop the bleeding and promote uneventful healing, so I begin to prepare for a major surgical session. I'm puzzled when I can't find the disposable razors in the cupboard where I knew I'd put them when I unpacked the stores earlier in the week. I enlist PW's help and, after he's looked and can't find them, send him to get some from my flat.

The next morning, mystified about the razors, I ask Margaret.

'Oh,' she says, 'I thought we were using too many. I wondered if someone was taking them from the cupboard, so I hid them.'

'But I needed them! If you're going to "hide" things, you need to tell me. I sent PW to get some of mine.'

'Well,' she says, 'that's very bad policy. You shouldn't give people the key to your flat. Anyway, you should've come and got me to help, if you were so busy.'

'Oh, I managed just fine,' I retort airily.

'That's not the point.'

My frustration peaks when a state-wide trial of daylight saving begins. In the past, attempts to bring Western Australia's summer time closer to that of the rest of Australia have failed dismally; Western Australians were adamant they did not want the change. Now there is a new state government in power, and it is time to try again. One reason is that Eastern Summer Time is three hours ahead of the West, which creates problems for businesses trying to communicate across the continent.

'There's total confusion,' Margaret says at the end of the first week of the new trial. 'No one knows what's happening.'

The school, store and office had gone straight to daylight saving time on the official date early in October. They open and close an hour earlier than before and most people manage to get to work and school on time. If the store closes before people have done their shopping, that's too bad. They borrow or go without until the next day.

'I think we should open at the new, early time, and close at the old,' Margaret announces. 'Otherwise it's too confusing.'

I'm not absolutely clear who is confused and, although I disagree, I decide it's better not to argue, for the sake of collegial harmony. Patients begin to arrive an hour earlier than before and continue well after the new clock-time closing hour. Still recovering from my stint of staffing the clinic alone, I find it difficult enough to work extended hours that include on-call duties at night and on weekends, without the added burden of increased 'official' hours. I also hate the assumption that the Martu people can manage the rest of their lives but when it comes to health care, they need to be cosseted and pampered.

An unexpected, welcome break comes, at Margaret's instigation, when I organise a major expedition to Port Hedland, a drive of six solid hours to the coast.

'Get the hospital to make as many appointments as you can over one or two days,' Margaret instructs. 'Then load everyone who has to see a consultant into the ambulance and drive them all to Port Hedland. It'll save air fares, and you'll hear first-hand what's happening with their medical treatment.'

'One of my sisters will give you a hand,' Joannie contributes. 'She's going to the eye specialist. She'll help with the old fellas.'

'Good idea,' Margaret agrees. 'She's a great help. She wants your job, doesn't she, Joannie?' she adds slyly.

'Yo. But no chance of that,' Joannie grins.

It is still dark when I drive cautiously into the camp to collect my passengers. The headlights shine on mounds of sleepers lying in family groups on the ground and on mattresses dragged into the open. People shift in their sleep as I drive past and dogs that never waste an excuse bark, snarl and growl at the intrusion.

The woman who is to help is dressed and waiting when I get to her place.

'Good morning,' she greets me, climbing into the passenger seat. 'I'll tell you where to go. It will be easier for you to find everyone that way.'

She directs me around the settlement, pointing out where everyone lives. She gets out, kneels, shakes them awake and urges them to get up. They stumble to the ambulance still groggy with sleep, in the clothes they've slept in. They organise themselves in the back on the stretchers along the sides before they doze off again, leaning heavily against each other. There has been no time for breakfast, even if they've thought about it.

By six-thirty, we are on the track to Newman, bumping over the corrugations in soft yellow light. An old woman with no teeth and no English holds her husband's hand tightly. I have noticed her leading him around the settlement. He is the older of the two, straight and tall with a stained cloth hat permanently on his head. Opaque cataracts have grown on both of his eyes. Apart from accepting her help as his perfect right, he ignores his wife. She bears his indifference and demonstrates her adoration through solicitous attention.

A twelve-month-old girl with a persistent kidney infection needs specialist diagnosis and treatment. Her plump, smiling mother, who is about seventeen years old, holds the baby constantly in her arms or else passes her to the other adults, and they play with her endlessly. A pregnant woman with an appointment to see an obstetrician about her elevated blood pressure takes particular delight in playing with the baby.

I hope the hospital will keep the expectant mother in Port Hedland. Taking her back to Jigalong with complications late in pregnancy would be like carrying a time bomb that was due to detonate. After my first panicky few days at Jigalong, when I'd been so nervous about delivering a baby by myself, I've learned that pregnant women are discouraged from staying at Jigalong after about six months' gestation, so that obstetric crises are rare in the settlement. Instead, the women go to Newman or Port Hedland, where they stay with relatives and give birth in the hospitals. Most of the young women seem to acquiesce to this even though it means their babies are born away from their own country and away from their kinsfolk.

I plan to drive about halfway before stopping for fuel and an early lunch at the Auski Roadhouse in the Karijini National Park. That way we'd arrive in Port Hedland in time to find the Aboriginal hostel before dark. It's a sensible plan, efficient and unambiguous. But my passengers have an entirely different view of travelling.

'Stop! Stop!' the woman on the seat beside me squeals as we pass the first roadhouse, a couple of kilometres from Newman.

I brake sharply and those in the back fall together in a heap, laughing.

'What's the matter?' I ask, alarmed.

'Time for tucker,' the woman says.

'Of course,' I reply. 'Sorry. I forgot you haven't had breakfast.'

This provokes more laughter, although I can't work out what I've said that was funny. I drive carefully onto the apron of the roadhouse and park out of habit in the only bit of shade near a stunted tree. They pile out and wander into the shop, where they prowl around among the counters and stand against the heated displays of takeaway food. It takes a long time to choose breakfast snacks and to be served. They change their minds often, but the woman behind the counter is patient. This roadhouse is well patronised by Martu travellers. The woman knows some of the Jigalong mob by name and they make shy jokes with her.

We stand around on the verandah while I drink dreadful instant coffee made from a secret recipe known exclusively to roadhouse proprietors and their staff. Already there's a sting in the sun and I'm glad to get back into the air-conditioning. The warm, heavy smell of chips and greasy sausages fills the vehicle.

People share what they've bought, taking a bite from this and a bite from that brown-paper-bag-wrapped delicacy until it's finished. Spirits are high now everyone has eaten, and my passengers settle down happily to snack on potato chips and Twisties, lollies and chocolate, and to suck and slurp from their cans of Coca-Cola. Until the next roadhouse.

Progress is slow: we stop at every opportunity between Newman and Port Hedland to restock the collective larder. I think half-heartedly about giving a community nurse speech about nutritious diet and healthy eating choices. After all, part of my job is to educate people in health matters.

But I'm reluctant to be a spoilsport. This journey is a welcome break from the routine of camp life for everyone else, and it feels like a holiday to me. It must be the usual way the Martu people travel, I think. When they go on their treks to the towns and other settlements they must take advantage of all the shops and stops along the way. They won't take any notice of me if I lecture; I'll spoil their fun, and put yet another barrier between us. I make up my mind to enjoy this jaunt with them and to have as much fun as I can.

Port Hedland is baked in the afternoon sun, but I'm astonished at its greenery. When the plane landed two months earlier I'd been appalled at the red dryness. Now, later in the year when it should be even drier, the trees and lawns outside the houses seem like a green miracle after the desert. Bougainvilleas hang over fences everywhere and wave long plumes of audacious colour in the air.

Without fuss my helper directs me past the hospital to a side street and the Aboriginal hostel. The minute I see it I'm pleased I've stood my ground and declined the suggestion of the clerk at the Newman Hospital that I should stay there, too. She's responsible for patients' travel and, like other bureaucrats in the Pilbara, she was keen to save money.

'Why don't you want to stay there?' she'd asked. 'The government will pay for it.'

'I'm craving the luxuries of civilisation,' I told her. 'A motel with a pool where I can wash away the desert dust. A meal I choose from a menu.'

'The government can't be expected to pay for a motel,' she said as if I was asking her to pay for my accommodation from her own bank account. 'You'll have to pay for it yourself.'

'I'd like to spend an evening without being interrupted and a night without being woken. I'll happily pay for that,' I said.

I could swear I heard her sniff at the other end of the phone.

'Suit yourself, then,' she said briskly.

She'd once admitted she'd never been to Jigalong. When I see the Aboriginal hostel in Port Hedland, I can tell she's never seen that, either.

It is a long, low, makeshift fibre-board building with what looks like an asbestos roof. A couple of old fellows sit on the verandah staring silently into middle distance until the old man with us greets them. Then they all talk together in language, often at the same time.

'Hi, there. Did you have a good trip?' the hostel manager greets us kindly. 'Now, who have we here?' She scans the clipboard she's holding and begins to work out who is who.

'I'll show you your rooms. Dinner's at six.'

The tour doesn't take long. Apart from two dormitories each with six beds, the other four rooms are cell-like; they're uniformly furnished with a camp stretcher and a packing case under a small window that has a shutter but no glass or wire screen. On each of the packing cases sits an empty unwashed ashtray and a jam tin of water. For drinking? I ask myself. The stretchers have fresh white sheets and old grey blankets folded at the end. There's no air-conditioning and the atmosphere reeks of cabbage, cigarette smoke and unwashed bodies. The bathroom is in a separate building accessed under a grey wooden trellis that looks as if it might shed another of its slats any minute. The bathroom smells of the urine and mould familiar in aged care facilities everywhere.

'This is your room, Sister,' the manager says, opening a door into one of the cells.

'Thank you,' I say. 'But I plan to stay at the motel.' I don't want to hurt her feelings by refusing hospitality, but I can't stay here. 'I'd hoped the clerk at Newman would have told you.'

'That's OK, luv. I understand.'

The other women look appalled.

'We're too scared to stay here without you,' one of the women whispers. She looks around fearfully.

'Yes, let's come with you.' Another woman pulls on my arm. They don't tell me what they're afraid of and I don't ask. I can't contemplate a night here, on a stretcher that sags under the weight of its own bed linen. I'd be happy to be with the women overnight, but paying for motel rooms for them is impractical.

'The Country Women's Association has a nice house in town,' the manager says, rescuing me. 'They use it for emergency accommodation. You women could stay there and the men can stay here. The rate's pretty reasonable. Shall I find out if it's available?'

She must have seen my relief because she smiles widely and goes off to the phone without waiting for a reply.

The pleasant house is in the older part of Hedland. Members of the Country Women's Association have furnished it with a well-stuffed, three-piece lounge suite and a heavy dark-wood coffee table on patterned carpet in the sitting room and a laminex table flanked by eight vinyl-covered chairs in the kitchen. Each of the single beds and the white-painted iron cot has a homemade patchwork quilt spread over ironed sheets and pillowcases. Posies of artificial flowers sit on embroidered doilies on each bedside table under reading lamps with handmade shades.

The women from Jigalong scream and coo as they bounce like children on the beds, while the baby I've carried in from the vehicle clutches my shirt in fright. Soon she's distracted by the silver snail at my neck. She puts it into her mouth with chubby fingers and sucks and chews it with the six incisors she flashes when she smiles. We choose our rooms and go to find the shops before they close.

The shopping mall with its choice of supermarkets is like paradise after my self-imposed deprivation. I've never before known that choosing between Coles and Woolworths could give such joy, and I'd forgotten the pleasure of walking along aisles of fresh fruit and vegetables. The plums, peaches and nectarines displayed in artistic piles under the bright colour-enhancing lights make my mouth water. I fill plastic bags with fruit and quickly select meat and vegetables and cereal and milk for breakfast. Before I'm out of the mall I've finished my first bunch of grapes.

We've cooked and eaten tea and the baby has ended up on my lap. I hold a sliver of peeled peach to her eager mouth as I would if she were my granddaughter. She contorts her face at the new taste, but soon sucks the fruit and my fingers noisily while the juice runs down her chin and over her bare round abdomen, and down my arm. Her mother and aunties watch, amused.

'Hey, Sis!' the mother says. 'She like that, eh? First time. Only milk from titty and meat, all she eat afore.'

'It's good for her, too,' I say, pushing the bowl of fruit across the table. 'It tastes wonderful. Why don't you have some yourself?'

'We don't like that fruit, Sis,' the mother says. The other women nod in agreement.

I carefully put what is left into the cabin of the ambulance when we leave the next morning, but it's already rotting by the time we finish with the hospital appointments; I throw it in the bin outside the first roadhouse on the way home.

Not even the baby is awake when I creep out of the house and drive to the Catholic church we passed yesterday. Attending Mass was a regular ritual in my life before Jigalong and I miss it. I regularly read the prayers from the Sunday Missal I'd taken with me, and once or twice Jim Marsh and I prayed together, but I longed to be at the Eucharist with other Catholics. As soon as Margaret suggested the trip, I planned to find the church in Port Hedland and go to an early morning Mass.

A car approaches down a driveway behind the building as I drive into the parking area. It stops and the driver winds down his window.

'There's no Mass this morning,' he greets me cheerfully. 'The bishop's visiting.' He indicates the smiling man in the passenger seat next to him. 'We're getting an early start. We have to drive a few hundred kilometres today.'

'I'm from Jigalong. I haven't been to Mass for months,' I say, hoping he'll change his mind about setting off so early. 'I read on the noticeboard that Mass was celebrated at seven every morning. I was looking forward ...' Already, tears mist my eyes, whether from shock or disappointment.

'Sorry. There's no Mass this morning,' he says firmly before he engages the gears and drives away.

28

Margaret is on call and I'm enjoying the luxury of an evening to myself. It's a time when I can reasonably hope not to be interrupted. The phone rings and I answer it eagerly, anticipating a rare call from family or friends in Perth.

'Maureen, this is to warn you both,' Sandy says urgently. 'Tell Margaret, too.' Her voice is strained. 'Someone seems to have gone off his face. He's tearing around the settlement ramming into buildings and other vehicles. He was outside here a minute ago. He's using a four-wheel drive with a bullbar.' She rings off before I have time to ask questions. I suppose she is calling all the others who need to know.

I open the door to go to the adjoining flat. There's an unusual din coming from the settlement and lights are shining where I hadn't expected them. By this time, as a rule, everyone has settled for the night. But there are dogs barking, people yelling abuse and frightened children screaming. These noises are punctuated with crashes. I bang hard with an open hand on the fly-wire door of the other flat, making as much noise as I can.

'Sandy called a minute ago,' I say as soon as Margaret opens the door. 'Someone's gone berserk. Listen!'

She hesitates for a minute, then says, 'Come inside quickly.' She pulls me inside. 'Don't stand out there.'

Through a window we watch a vehicle approach with its lights on high beam. There's a loud crunching and tearing noise close by as it crashes into a building. The engine reverberates as the man reverses the vehicle and drives off again at high speed. Seconds later Sandy runs across the road towards us.

'I've been listening to him,' she says breathlessly. 'He's been driving around for ten minutes, running into things. I was scared. If he decided to attack me, he could easily break down the caravan with the bullbar on that vehicle.'

Sandy, Margaret and I stand in the dark on the verandah, straining to hear what's going on while we work out what to do.

'Ray and Ian are out of the settlement tonight,' Sandy says. 'It's up to us to do something.'

'Yes, but what?' I ask. 'What can we do?' I've never experienced anything like this and I can't imagine what action we could take. It seems surreal — one of those bad dreams in which no action seems possible. It's not so much a feeling of helplessness as of incredulity that such a thing can be happening.

'We can't take risks with so many lives,' Margaret says, resolutely taking charge of the situation. 'I'll ring the police in Newman, while you put the kettle on.'

'Yes, to both ideas,' Sandy agrees. 'But it'll take ages for the police to call the off-duty officers to the station and for them to be briefed.'

'After that, they'll have a long drive,' Margaret adds. 'It'll take them hours. It's times like this that you know how much we need a resident police officer at Jigalong.'

'People have been asking for police to be stationed here for years,' Sandy explains for my benefit.

'I think I'll call the RFDS, too,' Margaret says. 'There's nothing they can do, but we should alert them in case we need them later.'

When she's rung the police and I've made coffee, we turn off all the lights and go outside, mugs in hand, and lean on the verandah rail. I watch the road anxiously as my eyes become accustomed to the light from the half moon. I'm hoping the man won't come back this way again. Vehicle lights shine intermittently as other cars move cautiously around the settlement, and some folk are driving over the bumpy terrain into the paddock next to the health compound. It looks as if they've piled their entire camps on top of the vehicles. They seem to be heading towards the loop in the creek.

Now it is twenty minutes since we last heard vehicles move around. We don't know what is happening or where the unpredictable fellow in the four-wheel drive has gone. We settle ourselves for a long wait until the police arrive, filling the time with desultory conversation and several more cups of coffee. It will be three and a half hours before two police vans draw up outside the clinic.

As they stop, someone fires a shot. It's followed by a volley in quick succession. We count aloud, aghast as a gun is discharged twelve times somewhere to the right of the verandah where we've been sitting for so long.

'Those shots are from a high-powered gun,' one of the police officers says as four of them bound over to us. 'This is a really dangerous situation.'

'You women must go immediately to the clinic,' says another. 'Don't turn on any lights, and lock the doors after you.'

'And keep them locked, whatever happens,' adds the third. 'We'll let you know when it's safe to come out. We can't take any risks.'

The police officers push their vans off the road and half-conceal them behind a cluster of low bushes. They creep warily, hunched over, into the settlement. Obediently, we go to hide as we've been instructed.

'This is crazy,' I say after half an hour of sitting in the dark clinic. 'I hate not being able to see or hear what's happening.'

'I felt safer on the verandah, I must admit,' Sandy says. 'At least we'd have some warning if he was coming our way.'

'Let's go back then,' Margaret suggests. 'I'm hungry. We can make some toast. Anyway, I feel safer with the police here, in spite of what they say.'

We move across the compound back to the verandah. Although we still can't see what is going on we have the advantage of being close to our kitchens. We make more hot drinks by torchlight, empty a packet of shortbread biscuits onto a plate and resign ourselves for another wait.

The sudden sound of muted voices nearby scares us. We grab the torches, but don't turn them on, afraid of attracting attention with the light as we edge our way towards the voices in the dark. There are three or four vehicles and about thirty people huddled together near the fence at the back of the compound.

'Hello, there. Are you all right?' Margaret whispers as we reach them. She turns on her torch and shines it towards her feet like a night-duty nurse in a hushed ward, keeping the light close to the ground.

'We're very cold,' a woman says. 'And the kids are freezing. They've been whingeing they're hungry and thirsty, too.'

'We've been here a long time, from when we first heard the banging. It was hot then.'

'That mad bugger! We were scared. Our camps weren't safe, so we came here.'

Most of the men are not wearing shirts and the children and old people are shivering. Margaret and I go back to the clinic and gather up all the blankets and bedspreads and towels we can find. Then we go and take more from our flats. Meanwhile, Sandy loads a tray with bread and biscuits from both kitchens and fills two litre containers with drinking water.

'This'll be better than nothing,' Margaret says when the three of us return to the makeshift camp. 'I'm sorry we don't have more blankets.'

'Much better, thanks, Sis. We can wrap ourselves in them and hug close together with the dogs. We'll be warm then.'

It is three o'clock before we see a police officer running with a torch along the road towards us.

'We've found him,' he calls breathlessly as soon as he's within hearing distance. 'He's on a mattress in the camp. We don't know if anyone's injured. Can one of you nurses come with me, please?'

'We'll all come,' Margaret says decisively. 'We'll stick together.'

'OK. That sounds fair enough,' the officer says. 'I'll just be a minute. I'll get the paddy wagon.'

He rattles his keys cheerfully as he walks back to the bushes. We go to the clinic again, this time to collect a first-aid box to take with us. Once past the health compound driveway, the van proceeds at walking pace, its lights now on full beam. We fall in behind it, walking sedately abreast like chief mourners following a hearse. The driver leads us to the end of the settlement where the lights pick out a man half-sitting on the ground outside a hut. There's someone on a double mattress next to him. They're surrounded by the three other police officers and a couple of grave-faced elders.

As we get closer I see the man has a captive. He has wound his hand in her long hair, and placed it on her face. Horrified, I notice that he's resting much of his probably 105-kilogram weight there. She lies still and silent, obviously too terrified to move.

'He's using his wife as a hostage,' Margaret says. 'Oh, the poor little thing!'

We watch helplessly until the police sergeant orders the man to let the woman go. Eventually he relinquishes his hold on her hair and sits up. Two officers attempt to restrain him and the others help the woman to her feet and bring her to where we are standing. She's shaken and shamed, her shoulders slumped. The man struggles violently and resists arrest with his considerable might. The police are dogged in their attempts to get him under control. He throws himself around, hitting the ground. People tie his feet together with a sheet, but still he jerks and bucks on the dirt.

'Let's put his mattress on the floor in the back of the paddy wagon,' Margaret suggests. 'That way, if he struggles when they get him in, he won't get hurt so badly. And he'll be exhausted after such a night. He might sleep quietly.'

'My wife must come with me,' the man insists when he finally capitulates.

'OK,' agrees one of the officers without consulting her. 'She can come.'

She steps forward and goes to him without a sound, and the man grabs her arm and pulls her close.

As soon as the door of the van shuts on the couple, Margaret and I relinquish the roles of bystanders and revert to our community nurse personae. We scurry back to the clinic and pack an ice box with the specimens of urine, blood and pus from the refrigerator, ready to send them to the pathology department in the hospital. We hear the police vans coming closer and Margaret darts outside and holds up her hand to stop them, while I trot along behind.

The first vehicle slows and the officer in the passenger seat winds down his window.

'Thanks for your help, girls,' he says. 'You did a good job tonight.'

I'm too tired even to complain about his language. Somehow it doesn't matter now that this young man calls us girls.

'Can you take this to the hospital in Newman, please?' Margaret thrusts the ice box towards the window.

'What's this?' he asks.

'Just stuff for pathology.'

The police officer hesitates, suspicious of the box she proffers.

'They're routine samples for processing,' she says impatiently. 'But they need to get to the hospital as soon as possible. Without spilling.'

He accepts the box gingerly and stows it on the floor under his feet.

'Thanks,' Margaret says.

It is six o'clock by the time the police vans roll away. Margaret and I go home for breakfast and a shower, then back to work for the day. Only the clinic opens. The school, store and office remain closed and most of the Martu people sleep. During the morning I take photos of an almost demolished hut and the only public phone box in the settlement, showing a bullet hole where a shot has gone through the glass. The police will confiscate my camera when they come back to assess the damage a few days from now. When they return it weeks later, the film will have been removed. In the envelope that accompanies the camera will be several prints of women posed inelegantly in the group room — a snapshot of the aerobics class I'd taken and forgotten.

'How could the rest of the whites not have heard the commotion?' Margaret wonders aloud.

'I feel let down. They left us to deal with such an enormous drama by ourselves,' I reply.

In the afternoon, after they've rested, the Martu tell us that everyone had run for safety, out of the camps and into the surrounding country.

'My mother hasn't walked for years,' the environmental health worker says. 'But last night, she run!'

'I run along the creek,' another man tells us proudly. 'I carry three kids. Lucky the creek dry!' He grins nervously at the memory.

Old women and men hobble to the clinic for bandages. They display their knees, hands and elbows, grazed when they fell on the gravel in the rush to escape. Other people reveal bruises and blistered and bleeding feet from their flight in terror from the gun, and from the person they now think of as a madman.

Recovering from the immediate effects, most members of the community are exhausted from their all-night vigil. Margaret and I take turns to sneak to our flats for an hour's nap in the afternoon, and we toss a coin to see who will be on call, but we are confident no one will wake us for a night or two.

In any other part of Australia, a siege by an armed gunman would have made headlines across the nation. A trauma team would have moved in to counsel everyone. Employers would have visited the scene. But the outside world never hears about Jigalong's night of terror.

29

A sudden personal emergency caused Margaret's second departure just three weeks after she'd returned from her holiday, and again I was the sole nurse in residence at Jigalong. By then, I'd become more proficient. I belonged. The thought of being alone was now a challenge, rather than a threat.

'I had hoped for the week's leave that's written into my contract,' I tell my supervisor in a phone conversation to Port Hedland soon after Margaret left. 'Will I be replaced?'

'Not a chance,' she laughs. 'With one nurse away, and we don't know how long for, you'll have to stay.'

'Oh! Well, put me on the list for leave as soon as you have a replacement then.'

Every year in early summer Martu people from different settlements, towns and outstations gathered for a big meeting, known as Law Business. It was a special time of religious ritual and ceremonies to celebrate the activities of the Ancestral Beings in the Dreaming, when they had created the land and set in place the laws and customs essential for the continuation of the spiritual, social and economic life of the tribe.

The preparation of young men for full participation in Martu adult life took place over a number of years and included ceremonies during Law Business. Initiation included the teaching and learning of important sacred knowledge available only to men, as well as circumcision. Women had their own secret rituals to perform in compliance with the Law, and the preparation of girls for womanhood. Law Business was often the time for the administration of ritual punishments for misdemeanours, and it helped to restore harmony in the community.

Because people from different language groups had been attracted to Jigalong and settled there, it was where Law Business was frequently (although not always) held. The non-Indigenous residents were convinced that Law Business would not be at Jigalong the year I was there. They believed that everyone fit to travel would go somewhere else. I was disappointed by these predictions because I'd hoped to see as much as possible of Martu culture. But the white people were wrong, and no one was prepared for the influx of people, twice as large as for the funeral a few weeks before, that occurred early in November.

The first trickle became a torrent as convoys of vehicles of many descriptions, all laden with human cargo, arrived from Newman and from other places many hundreds of kilometres away. Within a week the population increased to around a thousand people. Some camped with relatives and friends in the middle of the settlement. They pulled mattresses and pillows from vehicles and staked a claim to space in and around the dwellings of their brothers and sisters, aunts and uncles. The squalid accommodation, already too small and overcrowded, somehow expanded to make room for the newcomers.

Other people set up separate camps on the outskirts of the settlement, mostly on the hill near the old people. They used whatever they'd brought with them to make temporary dwellings, and slept in station wagons and on the backs of trucks. Everywhere, men wore red headbands around their foreheads. Like the one worn by PW, the bands were made from knitting wool or scraps of fabric, a tribute to Western culture. Some newcomers, especially those from the outstations, looked unkempt and scary.

The people from the outstations were mostly former residents of Jigalong, with strong social and financial ties to the community. They'd moved away to the new, less permanent settlements for family or social reasons, often in an attempt to be closer to their spiritual country. Others hoped to remove their children further away from the influence of alcohol and other attractions and temptations, or to avoid conflict. The outstations had no electricity, phones or stores and they had no schools or nursing posts. Some of the families moved regularly between Jigalong and the outstations according to the seasons, creating a circular movement in and out of each place.

While the Martu residents planned and organised resources for the big meeting, the influx of visitors stressed the infrastructure of the settlement, which was the official administrative centre for the outstations and a gateway to them. The single public phone was out of order, jammed with coins that no one collected. Local children no longer attended school. They ran around unsupervised and got into mischief. More walls were defaced with graffiti. Growing things, including a few silverbeet and tomato seedlings I'd planted and carefully nurtured in a tiny vegetable garden at the back of my flat, were pulled up and thrown on the ground where they dried out in the hot sun within an hour.

Taps were left running. The toilets in the public ablution blocks soon flooded as the septic system, sensitive at the best of times, broke down completely. The store ran out of food and although Ian made several trips a day in the truck to Newman, everything was sold within hours of the shelves being restocked. Sally's clothing store traded briskly. She'd managed to stock it with T-shirts printed with outlandish pictures and slogans and these were highly prized and worn everywhere. Even some of the sarongs, considered decoration by the locals, disappeared from the walls.

Queues of people waited for medical or nursing attention. What was always a heavy workload increased until the clinic was chaotic. People from outstations came with old injuries and chronic conditions for which they demanded new prescriptions or additional medication. They brought their toddlers and babies to be weighed and measured and for immunisation. They brought their old people whose vision and hearing and chests were failing. A small number came to use the shower and toilet on the outside of the clinic until they too became overloaded and the waste flooded onto the grass where it lay in filthy pools. Too busy to clean the toilet or to fix it, I put an 'Out of Order' sign on the door, which had no lock.

Women and older men found the clinic congenial and came for the company and the air-conditioning, especially as the clinic was one of the few buildings that had continuously cold air. Adolescent girls, urged on by the locals, asked to watch the videos about conception and childbirth. The videos played over and over in the group room and the young women giggled together. Young men demanded tests for each other for sexually transmitted diseases and came to be patched up after they'd been in scraps and fights.

Mothers ran water in the trough on the back verandah. Children and mothers shrieked with pleasure as the babies played in the communal bath, splashing themselves and everyone else. The women demanded towels that I supplied from the clinic's meagre supply. When they'd dried their babies they laid the towels in the sunshine for recycling. I had no time to wash and dry them properly for the next clients.

For several days, Joannie didn't come to work.

'Her son's been grabbed,' PW said hesitantly. 'He's been taken into the bush by the elders because it's time ...'

Joannie had an integral role in the initiation of her son. She and the other mothers were expected to cook for the men and boys involved in the ceremonies. PW, too, had a part to perform in Law Business, and his attendance at the already understaffed clinic for those two weeks was sporadic.

Joannie's sister invited me to watch the women's dances one night, but she didn't follow up the invitation. I waited until late and felt disappointed when I realised that she hadn't come to get me and I'd missed the occasion. I wondered if perhaps I hadn't shown enough interest when she asked, but I was learning to navigate a fine line between being under- and overenthusiastic.

Just before sunrise most mornings, when the air was still relatively cool and fresh on my skin, I walked for an hour or so before work. Sandy, under a wonderful pale pink Akubra that I coveted, often came with me. We sometimes borrowed a dog that Ian had adopted. She was a tame, well-fed dingo with soft yellow fur and mournful brown eyes. She was regularly confined in a fenced compound away from the camp dogs, but enjoyed being out and walking with humans as much as the next dog. She bounded along in front of us and ran back when we called or whistled, her tongue lolling and her features relaxed in a parody of a smile. Every day we walked along the track leading from Jigalong towards Newman, or else out past the rubbish tip to the airstrip. Bored with these two routes, I started to think I could venture further without getting lost.

One morning during Law Business I collected the dingo and set off. The office was busy of course and Sandy wanted to start before everyone else was awake. There were some wild grasses and a few faded wildflowers growing along the sides of the track and, further away, three clumps of Sturt Desert Peas. The nondescript grey-green plants grew low on the ground and I hadn't noticed them before, but overnight they'd blossomed in a nimbus of spectacular scarlet and black flowers.

I left the track and walked perhaps ten metres to look more closely, deciding to take my camera the next morning and photograph the plants. Sturt Desert Peas were among the challenging seeds my zealous gardener-grandfather once germinated. As a little girl, I'd watched in awe as he'd coaxed the seeds to life by covering them with newspaper and putting a match to it so the seeds were scorched and cracked open, before he soaked and planted them. I knew it would fascinate my family, and especially my father, to see photos of these flowers growing so prolifically in the wild.

It's almost lunchtime. Four middle-aged women are in the clinic. I'm surprised they look so grave. They don't respond as they usually do to my greeting.

'This morning, you went in Man's Land,' one of the women says accusingly, coming to the point without preamble.

It's clear from her manner and the body language of the group that she's their appointed spokesperson. I'm immediately alert; they think I'm responsible for some serious transgression. I try to breathe deeply, but my chest is constrained and my pulse racing.

'We watched you.'

'Did I?' I answer, puzzled. I can't remember going anywhere, except along the track on my walk.

'Bad for a woman to go there all the time,' the spokesperson continues sternly. 'Extra bad at Law Business. Very dangerous.'

'I'm sorry,' I repeat. I'm mortified. I've unwittingly broken an important edict. I'm beginning to understand some of the significance of the Law and I'm disappointed they think I'd transgress deliberately.

'Was it when I was looking at the flowers?'

'Yo. We saw you looking.'

'If you saw me, why didn't you stop me?'

'You were long way off. We call and call, but you didn't hear. We couldn't come closer. You were on Man's Land.'

Sacred places and objects belonged to the Dreamtime. The words the Jigalong mob used for sacred objects were translated literally as 'forbidden', 'dangerous' or 'from the Dreamtime'. Men and women had their own secret-sacred objects for use in ceremonies and rituals. The dangers ascribed to these objects affected the uninitiated, including young people coming into contact with them for the first time, and the opposite sex. The objects were safely hidden in special locations around the settlement, where ceremonial grounds were also constructed before major rituals. To protect the uninitiated, the places were designated 'Men's Land' or 'Women's Land', and access was forbidden.

Later, Sandy told me about the sacred sites around Jigalong. She'd presumed I knew, and hadn't thought to mention them. She gave me a copy of the community's conditions of entry to the settlement, binding on everyone including teachers and nurses, tradespeople and government officers. One condition stated:

> DO NOT venture away from your accommodation or work area. There are SACRED SITES on the boundaries of the township. If you go onto these areas you will be required to leave Jigalong Community Inc. IMMEDIATELY. You will NOT be permitted to return to the community.

Somehow, this important document with its vital information had slipped the collective memory of the organisation that employed me and the nurse who'd handed over, so nobody had given me a copy when I arrived.

I waited anxiously for a few days, expecting every minute to be expelled from the clinic and the settlement. I was torn between being glad I might be going home and not wanting to face the ignominy of being thrown out. Nothing happened, although everyone would have known about my transgression. After a week, it became clear the community wasn't going to punish me.

I'd become desperate for exercise and the opportunity to get away from the small circle of my workplace, and asked respectfully for permission to walk out along the main road. I was grateful when consent was given. Conscious I did not belong there, that this was other people's country and that I must tread lightly, I walked in the middle of the track, making sure my feet never deviated, even by accident, from the road which was often so poorly defined. My path was well worn. I came to appreciate the most minute changes along that three- or four-kilometre route. The land on either side seemed intensely mysterious and I was eager not to trespass into secret-sacred Land, where I had no place.

30

Two boys shuffle and kick up puffs of the dust that's smudged their jeans and caked their bare feet. They watch from under drooping eyelids, heads bowed. For half an hour they've hung around the clinic. They're at that awkward age that heralds puberty, when boys' legs and arms become too long and uncoordinated. I recognise these kids from the school where I'm now a frequent visitor. They're among the oldest boys in the school, and although legally they should stay at school until they're fifteen, they won't be there much longer. Older boys have better things to do with their time than to sit in boring classrooms.

A recent growth spurt has developed the back and shoulder muscles of my timid visitors and next year they could be grabbed during Law Business on the way to becoming men. I watch as they push and shove at each other, play-fighting, half serious, making half-hearted attempts at approaching the door then retreating. The smaller boy touches the front of his jeans, gingerly pulling them away from his body.

School has been out for hours and other children are playing outside the houses and humpies of the settlement. The last of the young mothers has taken her baby home for the night and the old folk have wandered off along the road to their camps. I can hear the calls of young men and the thud of a football as they kick it from one to another in the middle of the road. The football field has lost its appeal since the official football season finished and everyone has begun to use the street for recreation again. These days only an occasional feral goat or donkey scuttles past the goalposts, chased by mobs of children. The thuds of a hard ball on bare feet are interspersed with calls of 'Mine!' and 'Here!'. One of the young men has a royal blue and yellow beanie on his head and another wears a sleeveless jumper in the same colours, but the rest are in undistinguished shorts and T-shirts.

While I wait for the boys outside to make up their minds about whether or not to talk to me, I fill the sink with hot soapy water and wash and clean the debris from the afternoon session — an ear syringe, a pile of stained, green plastic bowls, a tray and several old coffee jars which have been used for storing antiseptic. Methodically, I tidy up and put everything away. Slowly I mop the sink and rub without hope or enthusiasm at stains from lotions and potions and rust that have taken twenty years to build up. I hope these two young fellows are not going to detain me this evening. It's been a long day, and I look forward to going home to my tiny flat, a cup of coffee and a new novel, a gift sent from a friend in the city. They creep closer and closer, until they appear in silhouette in the doorway.

'Come in,' I welcome them. 'What can I do for you two so late in the day?'

'He's sore,' whispers the bigger boy, speaking on behalf of his mate.

'Sore?' I ask. 'Did he tell you where he's sore?'

'There,' says the patient's advocate, pointing at the other boy's groin.

'What happened to make him sore?' I ask, hoping for the delicacy and diplomacy that will be needed for a white woman to deal with a problem in the area of a young boy's penis.

'Might have done up zip,' my informant says laconically.

'Ow! That must hurt,' I say carefully. 'It's painful to be caught in a zip.'

They nod vigorously, relieved that I understand without too many words.

'Do you think I could ...' I begin.

This is too much for the smaller boy, who shakes his head in alarm and sidles out of the door. The other boy looks at me as if he wants to talk, decides against it, and follows his mate across the verandah, down the road, past the school and the store, and out of sight down the dusty road in the pink dusk.

They're waiting when I arrive at the clinic in the morning, sitting on the long bench on the verandah outside the door. There's no one else around for a change, and I invite them into the treatment room and shut the door firmly behind us.

The smaller boy is distressed. He's had a painful night, I think. He wouldn't have slept well.

'You both know that something has to be done about the zip,' I say in my best no-nonsense voice, acquired as the mother of six children — four of them sons — and perfected in school-nurse settings.

They nod reluctantly.

'I can't help you unless you show me.'

Slowly, gingerly, the boy undoes the zip of his jeans. I'm surprised that it slides. He tugs at the pants and pulls them down far enough to display another zip, complete with a patch of denim carefully cut out and firmly attached to the foreskin of his penis, which is swollen to treble its normal size. I can see immediately that because of the swelling it will be impossible to loosen the zip from its tenacious grip.

I will need to consult with the boy's father and perhaps his mother, if not with other male elders, and I don't expect it will be easy. My role as the community nurse won't be enough to balance my situation as a white woman. But before I even approach the family, I must first ring the Royal Flying Doctor Service to alert them to the possibility of a flight to collect the boy and take him to a hospital for surgery.

'Yup! Circumcision under a general anaesthetic is the only way to go in a case like this,' the duty doctor tells me cheerfully.

'I'll need to talk to the parents,' I say delicately.

'Of course. Ring us back when you've squared it with them.'

I hang up the receiver, thinking how much I'm starting to love the optimism of the outback.

The clinic has filled with the morning clients, but they nod quietly when I say I'll be back in a while. Leaving the boys on the bench, I close the door behind me and set off to find the parents. No one knows where they are, but a couple of people tell me helpfully that they think they've gone to Marble Bar. When I find the boy's mother she doesn't know, or perhaps doesn't want to tell me, where the boy's father has gone, or when he'll be back. She is shy and softly spoken.

We sit on the ground while I talk to her about her son's predicament and the solution I think might work. I don't tell her yet that I've discussed it with the RFDS doctor. She needs time to come to terms with this dilemma and to suggest her own solutions. She becomes even quieter, and sits pleating the hem of her skirt with her fingers. I can see she's shocked, not yet ready for her young son to be taken from her. I'd seen the dejection of other women whose sons had been taken by elders, sometimes from the classroom, into the bush where they would be initiated into some phase of the Law. The mothers seemed sad, but proud. For their boys, it was time to become men.

The woman says nothing for a long time, weighing up the implications of what I've told her.

'Please talk to the boy's uncles,' she says. 'It's best if you do it.'

Urged by the mother, the uncles eventually gather around and squat in a circle to listen intently while I explain the problem and offer my proposed solution. They speak together in language, looking at me from time to time and nodding.

'We'll talk some more and tell you when he can go,' says a middle-aged man, whom I know to be the biological brother of the boy's father.

Back at the clinic, I discover the boys have gone. As usual I'm absorbed in my work and the insistent demands of other patients. The boy and his family do not arrive.

After an extended lunch break, PW returns to work.

'It's almost time to go home,' I say.

'I need antibiotics, Sis,' he says, calmly ignoring my sarcasm. 'A whole packet, please.'

'The boy ...?'

PW is silent. I look at him, hoping he'll tell me more, but he averts his face. It's obvious the men have made their decision. I take a packet of an appropriate antibiotic from the cupboard. I hope it will do a good job of settling the infection. And I pray PW will do a good job of looking after the little boy out in the bush.

31

The forcible removal of many Aboriginal children from their families early in the twentieth century cast a dark shadow over Aboriginal communities. The 'science' of eugenics, which used controlled breeding techniques to develop species, including humans, had gained legitimacy nationally and internationally, although it was clearly a form of collective racism. In Australia it was perpetrated by misguided, though perhaps well-meaning, government officials.

After the Aborigines Act was promulgated in 1905, any Aboriginal child could be removed from its parents. Children born either as the result of sexual 'favours' provided by Aboriginal women for white bosses and stockmen or as a result of sexual assault were especially targeted by police officers and other officials to create what is now called a stolen generation. Children were removed from their parents and transported to Christian missions or to government orphanages, long distances away from their families and their own countries. There they were supposed to be educated to take their place within European Australian society.

Painful, forced separation of children from families resulted in the weakening of traditional customs of childrearing passed from one generation to the next through practice and example. Children removed from their familiar surroundings and culture into alien institutions would have been inadequately nurtured, not always through the deliberate intention of staff, but because the nature of institutions precludes them from nurturing. With no models of how good parents and families act, those who'd been placed in institutions would have had diminished resources to train the new generation in the traditional way.

Memories of that earlier, painful era must have flooded back to the community in 1990 when the Welfare Department removed two Martu babies from their mother, who lived in the Pumajina community on the edge of Newman. Social workers who dealt with the family alleged that the mother used excessive alcohol and when drunk had been violent, not towards her babies, but towards other people. The department declared the children wards of the state, and arranged for them to be separated from their family and from each other and fostered by non-Indigenous women in two unrelated families in Newman.

Members of the Jigalong community knew the trauma that resulted from such separation. They also strongly resented the interference that gave white women, strangers, the custody of Martu babies. They believed that the girls should be returned to Jigalong, where they could be nurtured and raised in the Martu tradition.

A year after they were removed, the Welfare Department decided in favour of a traditional upbringing on the condition that the girls could be well cared for by close relatives of their mother. A social worker brought the little girls, by then aged three years and eighteen months, back to Jigalong. They were placed in the care of their mother's aunt, who was a member of the Council of Jigalong Community Incorporated and well-respected by the Martu people. She'd raised her own family and fostered other children. In the past she'd been employed by several community nurses to care for the small children they'd brought when they came to work in the settlement.

The little girls arrived dressed in white party frocks, with white shoes and long white socks edged with lace. Most Australian children their age wore a pair of shorts and a singlet or T-shirt. At Jigalong none of the children wore shoes or sandals. Within an hour the dresses were predictably filthy, caked with the red dirt of the desert. The shoes and socks were soon lost.

Negotiations had taken place at a high level between the Health and Welfare departments.

'The children can only stay with their family in Jigalong as long as the community nurses monitor their health,' my supervisor told me during a phone call hours after the children arrived.

'That sounds reasonable,' I said. 'That's what we nurses do.'

'You don't really understand,' she replied. 'The agreement says that nurses — and I know you are there by yourself, and that's unfortunate — are to examine both children every day and provide written reports to me. I'll pass them on to the Welfare people.'

'Literally every day?' I asked incredulously.

'Including weekends.'

'What if their aunt doesn't bring them to me, or goes off visiting somewhere?'

'You'll have to go to them. It's extra work, but I'm sure you'll manage it. Anyway, there's no room for negotiation. The decision was made in Perth,' she said as she ended the call.

I resented the added burden. As far as I knew, no healthy children who lived with responsible adults were subjected to daily physical examinations anywhere else in Australia. I'd never heard of such a ridiculous waste of time. I felt as if the government departments were using me to perpetrate child abuse, to protect themselves from criticism.

The unwarranted intrusion into their lives distressed everyone. The girls cried when they came to the clinic and when I went to visit them at their aunt's house. I could only guess the kinds of treatment they might have suffered at the hands of other white clinicians in the name of care. Their mother wept and railed at me. She didn't want to be accountable to me, any more than I did to her. The aunt tried to conform to the letter and the spirit of the order, but she was often in demand in the community and didn't always manage to get to the clinic during opening hours. At other times, she came when I was frantically busy and had to wait. I made appointments to see them on Saturdays and Sundays as I'd been instructed, but it was often difficult for the family and it encroached on my limited free time.

When the older child presented with sniffles and a runny nose, symptoms that any sensible person would have ignored in ordinary circumstances, I found it tough to decide how severe her cold really was, and whether I should take any action. The role of de facto police officer sat heavily on me and the stress impacted on my life and work.

Leaders of the Jigalong community challenged the role of the Welfare Department as guardians of the children. As the children's mother was a party to the legal action, the Aboriginal Legal Service declined to represent either the community or the mother in their cases against each other, in case the service lost the confidence of Aboriginal people elsewhere.

Six weeks after the children's return to Jigalong, the Children's Court convened in Newman and the case was heard in front of Magistrate Timothy Schwass. The case and its aftermath were extensively reported in the *West Australian* in the first few weeks of November 1991, on a very rare occasion when Jigalong was in the news before the release of the movie, *Rabbit Proof Fence,* years later. An editorial in the paper, commenting on the sorry story, made the accurate observation: 'Finding a workable solution to deep-seated Aboriginal problems is one of the most sensitive and complex issues facing the nation.'

In an odd twist, the Welfare Department and the community argued on the same side, against the mother, for the return of the children to kinsfolk in Jigalong.

The department argued that the children's moral welfare would be in jeopardy if they were left with white foster parents in Newman.

'The children's self-esteem, self-confidence and whole identity as Aboriginal persons will be formulated from seeing other Aboriginal people in Newman,' social worker Susan Hill told the court.

'*Drunken* Aboriginal people — is that what you mean?' Mr Schwass asked bluntly.

'Yes,' Susan said. 'If the mother could give up drinking and change her lifestyle, the girls wouldn't need care and protection. There is more incentive for her to change if her daughters are at Jigalong.'

Jigalong Community Inc. called a non-Indigenous woman they introduced as an expert witness, to give evidence on their behalf. She told the court that 'The placement of Aboriginal children with white families has failed miserably in the past'.

Questioned, she said she was satisfied the foster parents in Newman could provide for the girls' *material* needs, but she predicted problems when they reached adolescence. 'The only thing ahead for these kids is trouble — emotional problems, insecurity,' she said.

In his decision, the Magistrate ruled that the children should no longer be classified as wards of the state because their mother had made suitable arrangements for them to be cared for by foster mothers. This relieved the Welfare Department of guardianship. The responsibility for the care of the children reverted to the mother, who made it clear she would return the girls to the foster parents. Although one of the white foster mothers was overtly jubilant at the end of the hearing, it seemed that no one else was satisfied. In a scuffle outside the court building, the children's mother attacked Susan Hill and had to be restrained by the police.

While the magistrate's decision effectively upheld the application of the Jigalong community, the case hadn't turned out as they'd hoped. Members of the community were devastated. They argued that the court had thrown the Martu people's cause for self-determination back thirty years. They sought legal advice, and took out an injunction that day to prevent the removal of the children from the care of the community.

Soon after she heard the decision, the lawyer who represented the children's mother sent a facsimile to the Welfare Department, asking them to organise for the children to be returned to its Newman office that afternoon so they could be returned to the foster parents. The community coordinator, Ray, made a statement to the media on behalf of the community.

'The Martu people feel very strongly for the children, and believe they should be brought up in a traditional manner,' the statement read. 'The community cannot deny access to Jigalong to the mother, because she is a Martu person. But as to whether they will allow her to take the children away? That will be up to the people of Jigalong to decide.'

When she became aware of the response of the Jigalong community to the news of the court decision, the lawyer approached the police in Newman. She suggested that the children's mother should accompany the officers on their fortnightly visit to the settlement, which was due the next day. The police declined to interfere on the grounds that it was not appropriate for them to intervene.

'The community has no legal right to retain the children at this stage,' the lawyer fumed. 'As far as I'm concerned, the Welfare Department has a moral obligation to return the children to town, because they took them away.'

The case attracted considerable attention state-wide. The government minister responsible for child welfare said that, although the lawyer's request seemed reasonable, it would be difficult to execute.

'How does she expect us to achieve this, when she argues in court that the department has no authority over the children?' he asked. 'Now she expects us to exert some authority and hand the children over.' While he conceded that his department had an obligation to facilitate the return of the children, he said it had no authority to force the community to do anything.

The next day, the mother, accompanied by a non-Indigenous couple from Newman, drove to Jigalong to collect her daughters. Ray and one of the elders stopped them at the gate and talked to them. As everyone at Jigalong had anticipated, the couple was refused entry to the settlement under the by-laws of the community. They did not have the written permission they needed. Ray told them the community had sought an injunction to prevent the removal of the children from the settlement. A decision was expected later that day, and he agreed to notify the mother as soon as it arrived. Ray also broke the news to her that the children were not at Jigalong in any case, but had been taken by her aunt to a funeral at another Aboriginal community a couple of hundred kilometres away.

The injunction was not upheld and the Martu community reluctantly agreed to the return of the children to their mother's care. She remained at Jigalong to await the return of her children.

Sandy and I were walking back from the airstrip around six o'clock the next morning. In the distance, we saw women wielding weapons and bashing the windows and bodies of vehicles with what seemed like superhuman strength. The mother of the little girls had apparently enlisted the help of her sister and they'd drunk themselves into a condition in which they were no longer able to make reasonable decisions. Instead they'd chosen to wreak major damage on almost every car, station wagon, truck and utility in the settlement. I was relieved to find the Health Department vehicles were among the few left untouched.

Later in the morning, about fifteen Aboriginal men and women, visiting from several other Martu communities, joined the sisters. Alarmed at the level of violence and afraid for our safety, Ray insisted that all non-Indigenous workers in the settlement should gather in one place, where we could protect each other if what appeared to be an incipient riot became even more dangerous.

This was the second time in a few weeks that I'd been confronted by violent behaviour that posed a serious personal threat. I was surprised I wasn't more afraid, but I found it hard to believe what I saw and heard. When Ray arrived at the clinic to drive me to his house, I quickly grabbed my purse and closed and locked the door. Until the police arrived early in the afternoon and arrested the rioters we sat around inside, nervously listening to the warlike noises that advanced and receded outside, but unable to gauge accurately what was happening.

We were not attacked. It's difficult to imagine how being together would have helped if there had been another outcome to the rage the group outside expressed. The doors and insubstantial walls of Ray's house could have been smashed and we could have been assaulted. Perhaps it would have been more prudent for us to have fled for our lives as people had done from other communities in the face of ugly actions by angry people.

In the Newman Court the next day, the sisters and the visitors were charged with alcohol-related offences, disorderly conduct, damaging property and taking alcohol into an ostensibly dry community. Most of those charged subsequently spent time in prison. The riot made headlines in Perth newspapers, and friends and family members called to ensure I was safe.

'It was exciting,' I told them, playing the incident down. 'But we are all fine. Some property damage, no one was hurt. I'm fine. The little girls will be returned to Newman later today, to live with the white families there.'

32

It is unusual for PW to talk with me about the general community, although we often chat about his wife and children, so I'm very interested when he makes a point of telling me there are some young men arguing. He doesn't say what the fight's about and I don't ask.

'It might be nasty later,' he says. 'They looking for a good fight, them fellas. They not from round here. Come from another place.'

'Thanks for telling me. Is there something special I should know?' I ask.

He doesn't answer, but I've been here long enough and had enough experience to know that if someone is badly hurt I'll manage somehow.

After PW's warning I'm not surprised when two men, strangers, come to the clinic and one of them bangs imperiously on the wall near the door. They're middle-aged, with the dishevelled appearance of people from an outstation. It's late morning and there's no one else around. I can't help thinking they've waited until I'm alone. I notice they've driven into the compound and their utility is parked right outside the door.

'Get the flying doctor now,' the older one orders as soon as he sees me. His voice is too loud and he's standing too close.

'Is someone hurt?' I ask.

'My son. He has a broken back.'

'Gracious. That sounds bad.'

'Very bad. Might die.'

'I don't think so,' I say. 'But if you bring him to the clinic, I'll examine him and find out how badly he's hurt.' I hope I sound calmer and more reasonable than I feel. My heart is thudding and my mouth's suddenly dry. These men look more angry than worried. I wish PW had stayed around. As usual I make an effort to breathe deeply and to talk slowly.

'When I know what to tell the flying doctor, I'll ring him,' I tell them. 'If I need to.'

They don't like this answer and abuse me in a mixture of a language unfamiliar to me and English. Their anger is unmistakable now, even though I don't understand the words.

'The government will fine you. You might even go to jail,' I lie in an effort to protect myself. 'It'll cost big money if we get the doctor's plane to come and there's not a good reason.'

They walk away muttering to each other and climb into their vehicle where they sit and look back at me from time to time. They're clearly unhappy with me. The man in the passenger seat makes a threatening gesture and abuses me once more through the wound-down window before they drive away.

They're back within an hour, reeking of alcohol, as if they've needed false courage to confront me again. This time they've brought a young man with them. He's in the back of the utility, lying on a mattress, pressing the palm of one hand against the lumbar region of his back. He moans and blasphemes when he sees me. The older men help him into the clinic where he climbs unaided onto the examination table. There's no visible bruising or tenderness when I touch him, and his movements lead me to think there's little the matter with him.

'You can take him into Newman,' I tell the older men. 'It's a good hospital; they'll take an X-ray and find out what's the matter with him.'

'No. Get the plane here. Get a proper doctor here,' the father says. He adds as an aside to his mate, 'Silly fucken bitch.'

'He can have an X-ray in Newman. They can decide if he needs to go to Port Hedland,' I repeat, standing my ground.

This exchange is even more uncomfortable than the earlier one, but in spite of the abusive language and their obvious anger, I'm not afraid they'll hurt me. They're probably concerned about the fight between the two groups of young men, and want the RFDS to take the young man out of the way until the anger settles.

They drive away at high speed, leaving a dust trail. It would have been sensible if they'd taken a letter to give to the hospital's X-ray technician but it's too late now. I'm surprised PW doesn't return after lunch, because by now he (and the rest of the community) would know there's been some trouble.

I'm locking the door hours later when the older men speed towards the clinic. The driver slams on the brakes and they both jump out and run unsteadily towards me. They are brandishing spears. I can see their anger has been fuelled by an even larger quantity of alcohol and this is a serious attempt to influence my decision. I can smell the fumes of the alcohol, which might have affected their gait but not their use of language.

They're roaring obscenities and waving the spears.

This isn't a time to argue. It's obvious they have every intention of spearing me. They probably don't mean to kill me, I think, perhaps only to wound one of my thighs. I freeze. As soon as I can move I turn quickly, overwhelmed with relief when I see I've left the key in the lock. My palms are wet with perspiration and my fingers fumble as I open the door. I throw myself inside the cool, relative safety of the building and slam the door behind me.

I can hear my assailants banging on the door and kicking it. None of the buildings at Jigalong is built to withstand such an attack and the door and the walls of the clinic are flimsy. The men could smash through at any minute. I snatch up the phone and dial the coordinator's three-number extension. Ray answers after two rings and I tell him my predicament, wasting no words.

'Wait there,' he says.

I think perhaps he hasn't understood. There's nowhere for me to go. I have to wait until he comes. Please God, let him hurry.

I stand motionless, listening. There's an unexpected lull, even more frightening than the noise. They're probably conferring, I think, deciding how they can break through to get me. But the racket begins again. If they were sober, they'd have had no trouble breaking down the door. Thank God they are so drunk.

At last, above the senseless yelling and the barrage of blows on the front door, I hear the drone of a four-wheel drive vehicle speeding towards the clinic. Ray's appearance subdues the men. They hand over their spears, like naughty children caught fighting behind the school shed, mumble something in my direction, and get into their vehicle.

'You OK?' Ray asks quietly.

'Yes, thanks. They didn't hurt me. But I was scared. More scared than I've been in my whole life,' I babble.

'Yeah. They can be a scary mob all right.' He scratches his head. 'I don't like it when they're in town. There's often trouble.'

'PW hinted at that. But he didn't come back from lunch.'

'I'm not surprised. He could get into trouble himself if it looked as if he'd sided with one of us.'

'Thanks for coming so quickly. I was terrified.'

'That's my job,' he grins. 'Rescuing damsels. But we'll need to finish this off properly. Tomorrow.'

'How?'

'Have a conversation with them.'

'I don't want to.'

'I bet you don't. But it's the only way. Let them see you can stand your ground.'

Ray arrives early the next morning. I'm afraid, and note with interest that my fear is not especially to do with the men and their spears, but more about the confrontation I'm about to begin.

'Don't worry,' Ray reassures me. 'They'll have slept off the booze by now. They'll be ashamed of themselves.'

We drive to the temporary camp the three have set up behind the old people's site, and Ray calls to the older men, who are lying on the ground. The young fellow is sitting by a campfire holding a mug of something steaming.

'Did ya bring some Panadol, Sis?' he drawls.

I ignore him, not prepared to get into another argument about his alleged injuries. The other men struggle to a sitting position. They're a sorry-looking bunch this morning, and not in the least threatening.

'Your behaviour yesterday was not all right,' I say. 'You had no right to speak to me like that, or to threaten me.' My fear has subsided, and my voice sounds surprisingly strong.

They hang their heads, ashamed and powerless, like little boys who've been chastised.

'Sorry,' they mumble in unison.

'The best thing you can do is get out of here,' Ray tells them firmly. 'Today. Now. Go.' He points dramatically towards the road out of the settlement.

'You did that well,' he says, when we are back in the vehicle. 'You needed to, of course. You'd lose too much face otherwise.'

Although the incident of the men with spears ended well, it heightened my awareness of the constant danger that surrounded white women in the remote settlements. Around that time one of the young teachers, a new graduate on her first appointment, found a man in her house when she returned after school. There were rumours she'd been raped, but these weren't confirmed, and the Jigalong community — black and white, leaders and employees alike — all declined to discuss the incident. The woman left the settlement the following morning and did not return. Housing arrangements for the teachers were reorganised so that from then on no one lived alone.

Just months before I arrived at Jigalong two community nurses, members of a Catholic religious order, were threatened with rape at a settlement in the Kimberley region, north of the Pilbara. They fled in the middle of the night, in the vehicle from the clinic, fearing for their lives. The Health Department, concerned for its nurses' safety, declined to replace them until the police and the court systems had dealt with the men, and the Aboriginal leaders in that community had made an undertaking to protect nurses who might be employed to work there in the future.

Articles appeared in later issues of the *Australian Nurses Journal* decrying the conditions under which remote area nurses lived and worked. The nurses' union demanded safety measures be put in place to protect nurses on Aboriginal settlements but there was no action taken and no follow up to their demands.

With Margaret away I was again on call continuously. Each time I was woken, I felt increasingly nervous and reluctant to answer the door, especially as everyone knew the flat adjoining mine was empty.

I rang the office in Port Hedland to tell them what had happened, but they already knew.

'My leave?' I asked.

'The situation's hopeless. You'll have to wait a while. Perhaps after Christmas. Sorry.'

33

I'm driving home after running my errands in town. I've dawdled too long in the shops, and I'm tired from today's trip and accumulated fatigue. The road is interminable and I don't recognise that clump of trees over there to the right. Perhaps I've taken a wrong turning, without noticing.

'Don't be silly,' I tell myself, and wonder if I've spoken out loud. There's no one to hear, I decide, so it doesn't matter if I've started talking to myself. I'm scared and the sound of my own voice is a comfort. 'I can't have lost my way,' my thoughts churn on. 'There are no side roads from the Jigalong track. Or are there?' I can't remember.

But now I've lost my concentration and can't recognise any of the usual landmarks. That low hill on the horizon seems different from any I've seen before, dark purple rising out of the redness of the flat ground. The sun is suspended above the horizon and the sky flames with orange clouds and dust. I don't want to be alone on this track after dark. I'd hate that, even if I knew I was heading in the right direction. This is dangerous country, even in daylight. To be lost here could be lethal. If the country itself is not harsh enough, there are too many strangers around this evening, Aboriginal folk I don't know. Some of them were drunk and violent in the settlement last night after they'd driven out from Newman to visit. They left again this morning and I saw some of them in the park and on the footpaths in town, drinking cheap red wine from flagons. They are unpredictable.

I check the rear-vision mirror, nervous about being followed but wondering if it would be better to have company or to be all alone. I wipe a sweaty palm on the front of my T-shirt, clutch the steering wheel and slow to a crawl as the wheels veer from one side of the track to the other. I swallow hard and wonder if I should stop to stretch and walk around until I'm calmer. I drive another few kilometres then stop the vehicle.

As I climb out, my skin contracts. The hairs on my arms and the back of my neck stand on end. I'm transfixed, wondering what's happening. Before I can work it out a willy-willy appears, twisting and twirling, a dervish in the distance. Then three or four more materialise, enormous spirals of dust like columns of fire in the sunset. They are in a line reaching high into the sky, dancing out of control, devouring the desert. I'm terrified, afraid I'll be consumed. I sense the presence of the supernatural — Ancient Spirits, Other Beings, God. I throw myself into the vehicle, slam the door and lock it as I start the engine.

Years later in Perth I'll experience the same awe when I'm talking with an Aboriginal woman whose baby has died.

'My man, my baby's daddy, has the wrong skin,' she will say. 'We shouldn't have been together; our baby should not have been conceived. We knew that. The night before she died, my man heard something on the roof of our house. We were scared.' She paused to wipe her tears and blow her nose on a tissue from the box I pushed towards her.

'Go on,' I said quietly.

'We thought it might have been feather feet. He was very frightened and got out of bed. Then he went in his vehicle, straight away to his own country. When I woke up in the morning, my baby was dead in her cot.'

For weeks after this conversation, I struggled to align this new dimension of spiritual belief with my own deeply held Catholic faith. When I finally stopped trying to confront this different reality with rational thought, I found my spirituality could embrace the new ideas and be enriched by them.

Back on the road I drive half-crazed with fear for what seems like hours but is probably no more than twenty minutes, until the familiar line of trees along the creek bed looms ahead in the high beam of my headlights. Hot tears stream down my face with the relief of being home safely, and I resolve never to be alone out on that track in the dark again.

That night an intense, dry storm envelops Jigalong, filling the world with the great sounds of thunder and a furious wind that forces grit through the cracks and crevices of the buildings. I sit at the table, watching through the window the flashes of lightning and the billowing sand, while I wait for the roof to be lifted off and tossed away. I try the phone, but it's dead.

Abruptly, after several hours, the turmoil gives way to unbelievable tranquillity. The swirling sand that pinged off everything in its path subsides. The air is clear. Spindly trees that minutes before had gyrated wildly in the turbulence become motionless, poised against the sky where massive aubergine-purple clouds slowly rearrange themselves in the intermittent moonlight.

The sudden quiet frustrates me. I had hoped for rain to wash everything clean and lift my spirits, and daily I've become more pessimistic. The cyclone season has arrived and clouds often gather, but for all their promise only a few drops of rain have fallen since I've been at Jigalong. There were discrete pockmarks in the dust where raindrops had landed and displaced the dust that rose into the air with the impact.

It is hard to believe, in spite of the stories I've heard, that it will ever rain in Jigalong.

'You should see this place after it rains,' Margaret had told me the day after I arrived. 'It's so green. You'd scarcely believe it.' We were sitting on the verandah of the clinic, enjoying an unscheduled coffee stop. 'And then the wildflowers come out.'

'Sounds good,' I said, trying to imagine the red desert transformed.

'The flowers are not like you see them down south. But they're fantastic. Different. For a short time. More coffee?' She wandered inside the building, and came back carrying a mug of instant coffee in each hand.

'But it's not all plain sailing,' she continued as if she hadn't noticed the break in the conversation. 'Sometimes the creek floods. Without warning. Especially when there's been a cyclone along the coast. Sometimes we get flooded in.'

'What's that like?'

'I've got some photos somewhere. I'll see if I can find them.'

'I'd like that,' I said, not expecting she'd have time to look for them. She'd been complaining earlier how much she still had to do to get ready for her trip to Melbourne. 'What do people do in the floods?'

'Oh, you get by. Essential supplies are dropped from a plane if it goes on too long. Or if we run out. No one starves.' She laughed, and seemed to enjoy the disbelief I made no effort to hide.

'Well, I hope there's not a flood while I'm here,' I said. 'I don't think I'd survive. It'd be like a prison.'

'Hadn't thought about it like that. But you'd manage. You'd have to. Just like everyone else.' She sipped her coffee and was silent for such a long time I thought the topic had been exhausted.

'There was a bad flood before I came here,' she began again. 'I was working further north. I've been told about it. Even the Martu said it was a bad one.' She was quiet again.

'And?' I prompted. I wanted to find out all I could from her before she left.

'There was an English nurse. On a working holiday. Looking for adventure, I expect. Thought it might be a bit of a giggle, something to talk about. Lots of foreign nurses come here for a few weeks or months. The department doesn't employ them. Not directly. The temping agency sends them. It's cruel. None of the poor things has any idea what it's like here.'

'I certainly had no idea, either. I don't know how anyone could imagine it before they got here.'

'No. Well, they don't stay long. Can't cope.' She sniffed and stared into the middle distance. 'Anyway, it's a tragic story. This nurse's mother came all the way from England to visit her. Came out here to the desert. What a shock at the best of times! Then the rain came and everyone was trapped for six weeks because of the flood. The mother caught pneumonia. She was very sick and the nurse was frantic. As you can imagine. The road from Newman was under water and in bad shape. Almost from the Jigalong turnoff. The creek was badly flooded, even if they'd been able to make it that far. The airstrip was under water, planes couldn't land, but they did drop supplies once or twice.'

'Don't tell me . . .'

'The mother died. Despite everything the nurse tried, radio instructions from a Perth hospital and a cocktail of antibiotics — all administered illegally, of course — the woman died. Poor old thing. But she wasn't all that old, either. More like our age. The nurse was very young.'

'What happened next?'

'Oh, I heard they buried her somewhere over in that direction,' she says, pointing down the road. 'They couldn't do much else. I don't think the grave's marked. If it is, I've never been able to find it when I've gone to look.'

'And the nurse?'

'She left soon after. Can't say I blame her. But, like I say, no one stays long. She'd have gone anyway.'

34

The interminable hum of the air-conditioner was a constant background noise, one I'd grown so used to that I didn't hear it unless I listened consciously or if something went wrong. One evening it developed such a gurgle that it reminded me of someone's terminal illness. The nearest electrical contractor was a two-hour drive away, so a little do-it-yourself investigation seemed appropriate. Standing on a chair I unscrewed the cover and prised it off, spluttering at the dust that fell out. When I'd cleared away the dust I found a piece of metal touching the fan. I twisted it away, reassembled the unit and turned it on, delighted at my cleverness when it hummed evenly again. It had taken half an hour to fix and by that time the air inside was unbearably hot and humid. Hoping there'd be a breeze, I went outside. A wall of even hotter air hit my face when I opened the door, but at least outside the air was dry.

A woman stands on the other side of the fence, holding a baby awkwardly over one arm. She waves to attract my attention.

Not another sick baby, I think. I'm too hot and tired to see another person. I've spent so long fixing the air-conditioner that I haven't had time to make dinner, even if I'd felt like cooking. It's only an hour and a half since I closed the clinic door, and the night-time parade has begun. I look towards the mother who waits expectantly, looking for help. I force a smile and will myself to appear friendly and calm. I remind myself to breathe deeply. 'If all else fails, breathe', has become my mantra. It calms my anger, panic, fear. And sometimes, it keeps unbidden laughter at bay, too, when levity is inappropriate.

'So, what have we here?' I ask as I walk to the gate to meet the woman. She doesn't answer. One glance tells me the baby is extremely ill. When I put out my hands the mother relinquishes the child willingly. The baby's skin burns where it touches mine.

'My baby has a bad cold,' the woman says, telling the all-too-familiar story. 'Been sick long time. Won't suck.'

I wonder why she hasn't brought the child to the clinic where I've been all day, but I bite back the retort on my lips; there's no point in being angry. It isn't the mother's fault I'm alone.

'Let's take her inside,' I say as gently as I can. 'Then we'll undress her and I can have a good look.'

The mother nods silently. In the fluorescent light in the clinic, I see she's no more than sixteen. She looks undernourished, a thin little scrap of a girl. If she's from one of the outstations or from Newman, I'd most likely have seen her when she was pregnant, but I don't remember her. It's strange she's here by herself, without any of the other women, without friends. I wonder where she's camped, who is with her.

'How old is your baby?'

'Dunno.'

'When was she born, then?'

'Three weeks ago, maybe four. I forget,' she mumbles, looking intently at her fingernails.

The baby whimpers as I undress her. She's long and scrawny, a miserable-looking little thing. She reminds me more of the baby kangaroos the hunters tore from the pouches of their slaughtered mothers than the plump breastfed babies from around Jigalong. The muscles between her ribs retract with each breath. Her eyelids are crusted and her nose runs; thin mucous wets her top lip. I wipe it with a tissue and she doesn't resist. Through the stethoscope, I hear her lungs crackle and wheeze.

I'm concerned because she's so young and sick. If she was a few weeks older, in better condition, I'd be more confident.

'She's very sick,' I say. 'We have to get her to the hospital in Port Hedland.' A flicker crosses the woman's face; it passes too quickly for me to read the emotion. She gives no other indication she's heard, but keeps her head lowered, her eyes averted.

'Port Hedland,' I repeat, moving a little closer, wondering if she has understood. There's still no response. She glances at her baby, and then resumes the inspection of her fingernails.

'I'll get the Flying Doctor. You can go on the plane with your baby.' Still no answer.

'Will that be all right?' I ask, losing the little patience I've mustered. She appears to process the information, apparently weighing it up to see if she has any choice. Or perhaps she wonders how she can escape. After a minute or two she nods, almost imperceptibly.

Most of the young people (and many of the older ones) relish the opportunity to fly, unless they're too sick. This young woman's reticence doesn't make sense. Taking her silence for consent, I busy myself with the phone. I'm proud of my diagnostic skills, now greatly improved, and my communication with the RFDS base has grown more professional over the last few months.

'I'll get back to you,' the on-call officer tells me when she hears the baby's condition. 'There's some thunder and lightning here but so far it's not too bad. I'll talk to the doctor and the pilot. I'll ring you in ten minutes.'

The phone clicks and I replace the receiver and begin to do what I can, glad the baby will soon be someone else's responsibility. The doctor will insert an intravenous line to provide antibiotics and fluids, and in Port Hedland she'll receive the around-the-clock nursing care I can't provide here.

'Hi,' I say as I grab the phone after the first ring. I expect to hear the woman I'd been talking to at the RFDS base and I'm surprised to hear a male voice.

'Is that the nurse?' he asks cautiously. 'This is the RFDS doctor.' I don't recognise the voice. 'I'm new!'

'Sorry,' I say. 'I should have answered the phone properly, even if I'm stressed. In any case, I'm relieved to hear your voice.'

My relief is short-lived.

'We've got a problem at this end.'

'Yes?' He's got a problem? I don't want to hear. I want him to be the solution to *my* problems, not pose his own.

'There's a major storm brewing. The weather bureau says it could be upgraded to a cyclone within an hour or two. We can't risk putting a plane up. You'll have to manage the baby without us, I'm afraid. Sorry.'

'But she's very sick …' I begin, pleading like a thirteen-year-old.

'I understand,' the doctor says, his voice honey. 'From the history you've given us, the baby does sound very ill. But I'm sure you understand the risk if we attempted to fly.'

I have to acknowledge it could be dangerous. But my mind races as I try to work out alternatives.

'Can you drive to the hospital in Newman?' the doctor asks. Then he corrects himself. 'No, that's a silly idea.' He pauses. 'Of course, it's out of the question. There'd be nothing you could do if she got worse, stuck between Jigalong and Newman.' I hear him rustling papers as he speaks. 'I'll get hold of Princess Margaret Hospital. The paediatric registrar will keep in touch. You can work with him. Or her.'

'OK,' I say doubtfully. I didn't expect this. I started off tired and grumpy and I anticipated a night with a novel, now I'm involved in this new drama. But I've worked with the major city hospitals before and those experiences have been rewarding, although city medical staff struggle to understand my position and provide realistic support from such a distance.

'It's just that she's very ill,' I grumble again. 'I'm scared she'll die.'

'Sorry.'

'We have to stay here for the night,' I tell the mother as I hang up. 'Then, in the morning when the storm's passed, I hope you can go to Port Hedland.'

She pouts, shrugs and turns away.

The registrar rings within ten minutes.

'You nurses and the flying doctor people do such a good job,' she says in a lilting young-girl voice. 'I really admire you, up there by yourselves. Working in the outback seems so romantic when you live in a city, but it must be extremely difficult. I really can't imagine it.'

'It can be exciting sometimes,' I respond. 'But there's nothing at all romantic about it.'

After some negotiation we plan a treatment regimen that means the baby will be as safely cared for as possible, given the range of potential problems.

'I'm at the end of the phone,' she says, 'and I'll talk to the consultant, so he knows, too.'

I need to be vigilant until morning. There are antibiotics, ordered by the registrar, to be given throughout the night. That's a relief, anyway. I won't have to make medication decisions myself. There are regular observations, routine in hospitals, to be made. Tomorrow will be another full day in the clinic and already I'm desperate for sleep.

I toy with my options but don't like any of them. I could doze in a chair, I muse, or make a bed on the floor in the clinic. The mother could sleep on the examination couch but it's very narrow and she'll want to sleep with the baby next to her. That's too dangerous; a baby in my care falling off a bed is the last thing I want. I could drag a mattress to my flat and let them both sleep on the living room floor. Sleeping in my own flat in a chair is the most attractive alternative. I'll use my alarm on low volume to wake me every hour to check on the baby.

I have no social framework for sleeping with clients or inviting them into my living space, and I'm reluctant. The thought of sleeping in the clinic revolts me. None of the choices seems professional, but I can't think of another way out of the dilemma. I won't be able to stay awake all night; the days when I could work all day and party all night have long gone.

'If you hold your baby,' I say decisively, thrusting the child at her mother. 'I'll get ready. We'll both sleep at my house and we can look after your baby there.' My voice is rough and I sound as ungracious as I feel, knowing I'm not giving her a choice. It's not what either of us wants.

She needs time to digest the information while I gather bedding and equipment we'll need from the clinic for the night. She touches my arm.

'Sis,' she says in a small voice. 'I need my friend.'

I'm appalled. Not only do I have to share my house with a client and her baby, but she expects me to accommodate other strangers as well. I'm in no mood to put myself in anyone else's shoes, and feel any last vestiges of compassion leach away.

'No,' I say, sharply. 'That's not possible. No.' My face feels like flint. At the time I'm saying it, I already know I'll regret this decision later, but I have other things to do.

35

I wake in panic, with the sun shining on my face. I've been sleeping deeply and I've lost all sense of the time. The sounds of another person in my space and the sibilance of oxygen from a cylinder are alien. Then I recall, I should see to the baby. I stumble wearily off the bed and remember I'd meant only to put my head on the pillow for a minute or two, when it was still dark. Through the window I see all threat of storm has passed and the sun is well above the horizon. Morning light caresses the chrome-green tops of the trees in the yard.

Over dinner a few nights before, I'd told Jim Marsh about my family and home in Perth, and about my new grandchild who was due in a couple of months. Homesick, I'd speculated about how a person would know it was time to leave Jigalong and go home.

'I think you'll know,' he'd said. 'There'll be a sign. The tamarisks will burst into flower or you'll be moved by a memory. Something of that nature. You'll know when it's time to go.' He smiled as he spoke, and I believed him.

The sun on the trees this morning is lovely, but I do not think it is *that* sign.

The mother lies on her back and snores gently on the mattress on the carpet, with the baby in the crook of her arm. She is young and vulnerable, a baby with a baby, too young for such responsibility. I wonder again where *her* mother might be, and her aunties and her grandmothers. I should have asked those questions the night before, found out more about her. It would be better if she'd had her family with her in this crisis. Guiltily, I remember my refusal of the company of a friend. That was cruel of me, unnatural for her. She wouldn't be used to sleeping alone with an outsider as her only company, and the strangeness of my flat will have compounded her apprehension.

Neither mother nor baby stirs while I stand watching. Predictably, the baby's breathing is still too fast, her breaths too shallow. I squat beside them and take her from her mother's arms. Her colour hasn't improved; she's a strange shade of grey. The little oxygen mask has fallen off and I put it back over her face without disturbing her or her mother. Several times during the night she has taken sips of boiled water from a teaspoon and once she sucked for a minute or two at her mother's breast. Her nappy is damp now so I know she's less dehydrated. But she needs more fluids this morning.

The mother wakes gradually, then sits up and smiles shyly. I feel forgiven.

'Good morning,' I say. 'I'm glad you're awake.'

She nods and raises her fingers from the sheet in greeting.

'Your baby's still very sick,' I say as I give the baby back.

The mother touches the baby's tiny face reverently. She's wearing a silver ring with what looks like an elaborate marijuana leaf decoration on her index finger, and a plainer ring on the thumb of the same hand.

'The weather's improved,' I say, nodding towards the window. 'Look, no storms today. The doctor can come and we can get you both to the hospital.' She says nothing. Instead, she gazes intently at her daughter who is now on the mattress between her mother's outspread legs.

'Be careful you don't spill it on her,' I caution as I pass her a mug of milky, well-sugared tea. 'It's very hot.'

She takes the mug and sips gingerly, and then sits attentively while I go to the phone in the bedroom and dial the Flying Doctors' number. I walk with the phone to the doorway where I can watch the mother and baby while I talk.

'We were just talking about you,' the officer says. 'Wondering how you're getting on.'

'We survived.'

'Good. So, you still want us to come?'

'As soon as you can, please.' I smile across at the mother, but she quickly averts her face.

There's no point in worrying about her response, I tell myself as I make a plate of toast and more coffee and tea and put them on the kitchen table with butter from the refrigerator softened in the microwave, and jars of jam and Vegemite. I'm starving. I haven't eaten since lunch yesterday.

My eyes feel as if half the desert has lodged under the lids and my head aches dully from a deadly combination that includes broken sleep and fear. I'm also triumphant. We've survived the night and the baby is alive. That's an achievement, another milestone on my journey towards being a remote area nurse. Help in the form of professional colleagues is on its way. Soon I can get back to normal — as normal as Jigalong allows, that is, with its constant capacity to surprise, shock and delight me. I take a deep breath and relax. The coffee tastes good.

'Breakfast's ready,' I say. The woman puts her baby on the mound of bedclothes she's just left, hitches up the jeans she hasn't taken off for the night, and comes to the table.

'Sis?' my companion says hesitantly when she sits opposite me. I look up, but she concentrates on spreading butter on the toast on her plate and declines to make eye contact. I make what I hope is an encouraging sound in my throat.

'Sis,' she starts again.

'What is it?'

'I don' wanna go.'

'Pardon?' I inquire. I think I've misheard, or perhaps she isn't talking about Port Hedland.

'I can't,' she says simply. She shrugs, and her oversized T-shirt falls off her bony shoulder. She holds out her hands in supplication. Or perhaps it's a gesture of defeat.

'But your baby . . .' I say. 'She needs to go to get better. Do you understand?'

She nods miserably. 'Yo. But . . . it's too far,' she says.

I don't argue, confident that arguing will get us nowhere. In the other world I knew, parents with a sick child did what they had to do to get the child better, even if it meant putting up with personal inconvenience. There's something else going on for this young woman, something I don't understand and she isn't telling me. I'm weary, not just from the night's broken sleep, but also from so much decision-making. The baby could die if she stays at Jigalong, and if she dies the mother and I might both be victims of payback for letting it happen. It seems simple to me. The plane with a doctor and nurse will arrive in a couple of hours. They can have a debate with the mother if she hasn't changed her mind and if they have the energy for it. I begin to tidy the kitchen.

Days later, when I reflect on this morning, I'll begin to understand. Then I'll experience deep shame because I've been reluctant to engage with the young woman. All I've seen is a critically ill baby, not a family unit. It won't occur to me until later that the mother might have another, equally valid story, one different from the scenario I'd imagined.

I check the baby before I go into the bathroom and tear off the clothes I've worn since this time yesterday. Hot water cascades from the shower, something I no longer take for granted. I'm grateful but spend no time luxuriating. I'm under the water just long enough to wash myself quickly and shampoo my hair. There's no time for conditioner this morning. I dry myself hurriedly and pull on fresh shorts and T-shirt. I give my hair a quick rub with the towel that I wrap, turban-style, around my head before I go to look at the baby again.

The room is a jumble with bedclothes heaped on the mattress with the pillows, and an empty mug in a pool of coffee on top of the television set. There's another cup lying on its side on the carpet near a pile of nappies. The oxygen hisses through the diminutive face mask, dropped on the floor. The antibiotic syrup and pipette are where I left them on the kitchen bench with the unwashed breakfast dishes.

The woman and her baby have gone.

I put my head around the door into the cubicle where I sleep, surprised to find it's as untidy as the living room. I didn't expect the mother and baby to be in here, but I have to make sure. I call, but already know she's run away so she won't have to take the journey she's said so emphatically she does not want.

Pausing long enough to drag the towel from my head and drop it on the floor, and to thrust my feet into a pair of sandals to protect them from the heat and prickles and ants, I run outside, yelling as I go. I run past the still-closed school towards the store, but I have no idea where to start looking. I'm compelled to keep moving, although part of me knows how fruitless, even absurd, my search will be if the woman is intent on not being found.

Two adolescent girls saunter towards me, deep in conversation, and I stop to gather my breath. They're amused to see the nurse running helter-skelter along the main street, her hair wet and uncombed, so early in the morning.

'Have you seen a woman with a sick baby?' I ask when they are closer. They shake their heads, smile widely and make no effort to hide their enjoyment.

'If you see her, please tell her to come to the clinic. The baby must have medicine and go to Port Hedland.'

I ask the other little groups I pass the same question until at last I reach Joannie's house. Joannie will help me, if anyone can. She'll know where to find the child and her mother. The morning is already hot and the wind blasts from the south-east, heralding another blistering day. The sick baby won't survive long in this heat, especially if she's not drinking.

'She's not here,' a relative tells me when she answers my urgent knocking. 'She's gone to the funeral in Marble Bar. Won't be back very soon.'

'Bother! I'd forgotten. Well, thanks, anyway.'

The earlier adrenaline rush that's propelled me has spent itself and I walk slowly back to the clinic. I'm the only one at work. PW has probably gone to the funeral too. I feel affronted that he hasn't bothered to let me know he won't be here today.

I make another cup of coffee and force myself to sit quietly at the desk. First, I think, I'll ring the RFDS, to let them know what's happened. It's too expensive for them to fly to Jigalong unless the baby is here. The little mother is probably hiding somewhere and she'll reappear any minute. But I can't rule out the possibility that she's hitched a ride to Newman or out to the Robertson Range or another outstation even further away. If she was determined to get away, it would be easy enough.

'They've already gone out to the airport,' the RFDS officer tells me when I call. 'I'll see if I can get a message to them. If they haven't left, they can ring you from there.'

This is women's business, I think. I'll find a sympathetic woman who hasn't gone to Marble Bar and enlist her help.

My neighbour is sweeping the path outside her camp.

'Hello, Sis,' she greets me. 'Cup o' tea? Damper? I made it just now. It's still hot.'

'No thanks. There's no time. Thank goodness you're still here. I need help.'

'Yo,' she says when I've told her the story. 'I'll help. I know that one.' She leans on the clinic broom.

'Thank goodness.' I'm relieved I no longer have to depend entirely on my own resources.

'I'll find her mother-in-law,' she says. 'We'll look for her together.'

'Will you threaten to flog her?' I ask. As soon as the words are out, I experience a deep shame that covers me like a pall. I do not understand what happened. Even in my anxiety, I have no right to ask a question like that.

'No. Not necessary,' my neighbour says gently. She turns to go into her house, but remembers something and changes her mind. She comes back to where I'm standing.

'You can have the broom back, too, by'n'by,' she says in a conspiratorial voice.

Within half an hour, my neighbour arrives at the clinic alone.

'We found them,' she says quietly.

'That's wonderful. Where are they?'

'The girl has left now with her man to go to her auntie's funeral. That's why she couldn't go to Port Hedland. She has to go to the funeral. She's left the little baby here.'

'Thank you, my friend. But where *is* the baby? She needs help, urgently.'

'Yo. She's in the little camp, over there. We left her for you. But hurry!' She points with her chin towards a hut behind the big shed where the bush meeting was held.

I set off at a run.

The door of the hut's ajar but the place looks uninhabited. The grey ash is cold in the hearth outside, and there's no evidence of recently eaten food. I push the door and peer into the gloomy interior of the single windowless room. My eyes take a while to adjust and my skin registers the temperature, hotter even than outside in the sunshine.

There's a slight sound, not quite a whimper. Surely it's not human? I strain to see what it is and find the baby girl, abandoned and motionless on a filthy mattress in the corner. I pick the child up gently, willing her to be alive, even though I've heard her whimper. My mind plays tricks. With the baby in my arms, I walk quickly to the cool of the clinic and run a basin of tepid water to sponge her, glad that I hadn't been able to cancel the flight.

By the time the doctor and nurse arrive to take my tiny charge to the hospital in Port Hedland, I've regained my composure.

'Her mother isn't here,' I tell them, deciding they don't need to know the details of how I've spent the last twelve hours, or about my frantic search for the young woman. 'She had to go to a funeral, and the baby was too sick to travel with her.'

'That's sad for both of them,' the nurse says, her voice sympathetic. 'I guess this little scrap has been breastfed until now? I'll make sure the staff at the hospital knows she's just been weaned. The poor mother!'

Together, the nurse and doctor prepare the baby for the flight. They insert an intravenous line and give her fluids and antibiotics before we all get into the ambulance for the familiar drive to the plane.

'Don't you worry,' the flight nurse says, walking towards the steps into the plane, behind the baby and the doctor. 'We'll take good care of her.' She smiles and waves at me before she closes the door.

36

There was some part of me — a part I have difficulty owning because it resonates with a mysterious dark violence within me — that was prepared to condone the use of any means available, even physical abuse, to control the young woman, to force her to conform to my idea of what was appropriate, even though it went against her conscience. According to the Law by which she lived, the obligation she owed to her dead mother's sister overrode everything else, even the possible death of her baby.

To let the baby die because I made no attempt to find her was unthinkable, and yet to coerce the mother to abandon her child under a threat of physical violence would have been a denial of one of the basic human rights in which I believe so passionately. Intent on saving the baby, or at least getting her to the medical attention I couldn't provide at Jigalong, my actions transgressed against everything I believed. I eventually came to understand, on a deeper level than ever before, why people excuse themselves with the phrase, 'for her own good'; but at that time it was not the young woman's good I had in mind.

Cultural differences, inexperience, lack of support, no recreation time, months of exhaustion and one final sleepless night contributed to my decision-making that morning. I strayed between the overlapping boundaries of the two cultures into a grey zone, one in which I forsook the cool professional demeanour I had trained myself to exhibit, and instead resorted to physical violence by proxy in order to obtain what I perceived was the best outcome.

Desperate for a break, anxious to be with my family and friends and to recover from the gruelling incidents I'd experienced, I asked again for a week's leave, the week already long overdue.

'There's still no one to relieve you,' my supervisor said. 'Can you hold on a bit longer? We know it's been tough. You can have leave just as soon as the next relief nurse becomes available.'

I did not see the tamarisk trees in bloom. I did not need their blossom as a sign that it was time to move away from Jigalong. Instead, in an unanticipated phone call a few days after the baby had gone to Port Hedland, I was invited to set up a relationship counselling agency, quite different from nursing, in Albany, a town far removed from the Pilbara, and I knew it was time for me to go. I knew, also, my leaving would mean that, although it might be difficult to find a short-term relief nurse, the Health Department would soon employ someone to fill a vacant permanent position.

Getting ready to depart, I bundled up the clothes and household linen I'd taken with me and gave everything away. I wasn't the first nurse to have left and the local women did not seem surprised that I'd abandon my possessions before I went. I emptied the kitchen cupboards and put the food outside the door of the clinic, embarrassed by the number of tins and jars and packets I'd accumulated, as if I'd been hoarding in case there was a siege or flood.

My farewells were perfunctory. Sandy was on leave in Perth and so was Sally. The teachers were away again on holiday and most of them had told me they would not return. Joannie and PW and the few other Martu people who had befriended me seemed sad that I was going, and I knew I'd miss them.

I left Jigalong, but there was no immediate closure, no happy ending. I hadn't done many of the things I'd hoped. I felt I hadn't made a difference to anyone but myself. Another nurse, perhaps one with specialist skills, more commitment, a different understanding, would come along soon to take my place. But there would still be impermanence about health care at Jigalong, a void or a lack that could not be filled by well-meaning nurses until or unless the impersonal systems changed.

I learned how much needed to be done in the area of white/black relations in Australia. I saw the futility of imposing sophisticated Western health, education and welfare systems on people who live in remote areas where they do not have even the basic utilities that the rest of Australia takes for granted. I saw first-hand the interrelatedness of education, employment, adequate housing and basic health care. When any of these elements is missing the others cannot succeed, but it seems that if we keep doing what we have always done we'll keep getting the same unhappy results.

It will take many decades and enormous goodwill on both sides to work out what the partnership between the Martu people and the wider Australian society should look like, but a good start would be the recognition of, and respect for, the vibrant culture which underpins the lives of the people, and an attempt at dialogue that seeks to understand the Martu viewpoint. Next would be the provision of basic government services to the settlement: a constant supply of clean water, a reliable sewerage system and dependable electricity and telecommunication services, like those taken for granted by most Australians. Access to the outside world via roads regularly graded might be necessary if Jigalong is not to remain an out-of-sight ghetto.

The community at Jigalong challenged my skills as a nurse and imposed a severe strain on my personal ability to cope.

Working day and night would take its toll on anyone, not just a woman at the far end of middle age, and I was tired when I left. But I came away knowing that, under pressure, I was capable of more adequate responses than I'd thought possible. The time I spent at Jigalong taught me a little humility, also, because now I know I don't have to supply the answers for other people's predicaments. I do know that when solutions to a complex situation seem clear-cut, I can be certain I have not fully understood the problem.

Epilogue

The suburban train is crowded in spite of its additional carriages. At each station people push their way in, to stand swaying against each other in the aisles, on their way to demonstrate solidarity with hundreds and thousands of others, black and white, in cities across Australia. The crowd is casually dressed in jeans and shorts and T-shirts; their sneakers and sandals are suitable for the long walk from one side of the Causeway to the other, across the Swan River, and through the city up to Kings Park. The people push prams, carry bottled water and wear hats to protect themselves from the late-morning sun. There's a hum of excitement. Friends and acquaintances talk together good-naturedly and strangers exchange smiles. There's a common purpose, a common goal; we hope to demonstrate, by walking across the bridge, the sorrow that the Commonwealth Government has so far refused to acknowledge for past wrongs against the Aboriginal people of Australia.

Next to me, balancing on the seat that runs along the wall of the train, a young Aboriginal woman struggles with one hand to contain a toddler in a pusher. A little girl at her knee clutches her mother's skirt. The child's other hand holds a lolly that she sucks with a solemn face and loud slurping. On the woman's lap, a wriggling baby twists and bends, trying in turn to wrest the sweet from his sister, climb onto the back of the seat and get down on the floor. On the seat opposite, another young woman is engaged in a similar tussle with several children. From the way they talk to each other and to the children, I gather the women are sisters, or at least close relatives.

'You've got your hands full,' I say to the woman next to me.

'Yes,' she says shyly. 'This train trip's too long for the children.'

'Hey. Stop!' she says, and she bends forward to grab the toddler who has loosened the strap that restrains him and now stands rocking the pram dangerously. The baby on the woman's lap overbalances and lurches towards me. I put out a hand to stop him from falling, and clutch a handful of his shirt. He rights himself and grabs at the ring on my finger. I wiggle my hand and he grasps my index finger and tries to put it into his mouth.

It's my turn to feel shy. I look at the woman.

'Can I . . .?' I ask.

She nods and I distract him with a finger game of pat-a-cake. Aware of the onlookers, I quietly sing the melody that goes with the actions, enjoying myself as I play with this baby. He stares intently at my lips, and then puts out his hand to touch them. His podgy fingers smell of butter and Vegemite.

Before long he crawls from his mother's lap to mine and settles himself comfortably. He explores with his hands my face, earrings and grey hair. We smile at each other and I fall in love with his brown eyes and perfect skin. Finally he discovers the chain around my neck. He grasps the smooth, silver snail and puts it into his mouth, sucking and chewing on it, my child-magnet that has attracted children and babies for two decades. After all this time, I'm confident it won't break.

The mother watches and smiles gently at the two of us. She catches my eye, almost by accident, then bends down and lifts the restless toddler from the pram and sits him on her lap in the place the baby had occupied. The baby snuggles against my breast, where he dribbles; his saliva creates a dark, wet patch on my shirt. He closes his eyes, long dark lashes against his cheek, my snail in his hand.

We reach the station where we must change trains to connect with another that will deliver us closer to the start of the demonstration. The mother puts the toddler in the pram before I pass the sleeping baby gently back to her. He whimpers softly, and then nestles against her. She cradles him with one arm curved around his chubby body. With her other hand she grips the handle of the pram and a shopping bag stuffed with clothes.

'Hold on tight,' she tells the little girl. 'Hold the pram and don't get lost.' The women wait until the crowd disembarks before they manoeuvre the children off the train.

I follow the crowd that hurries across the platform to the next train, and jump on as the doors close. It is so full I'm left to strap hang and I bend my knees slightly to look through one of the windows. The women stand close together, surrounded by bags and children, the prams nearby, like wagons in a circle. I'd thought they were coming to the demonstration but perhaps I was mistaken. They've certainly made no effort to be on this train.

Twenty minutes later, I'm standing in another queue, waiting for the bus that shuttles people from the trains to the park at the start of the walk. Dozens of people mill around; they're less cheerful now. Some wish volubly they'd walked instead of waiting for the bus, others are anxious they'll miss the start and will have to walk across the bridge by themselves. Parents soothe bored children. Some fish in bags and retrieve packets of sandwiches, pieces of fruit and bags of chips that they thrust towards the kids.

The sisters from the train pass close to where I stand. We smile, greet each other, pleased. The baby, awake and energetic again, catches sight of me and smiles. He puts both hands out and I take him from his mother. Holding him close, I kiss the top of his head. She smiles at me. The crowd shuffles around us noisily, but now I'm at peace, grateful for the experience that was Jigalong that has so enriched my life and enlarged my heart. The urge to protest has dissipated, and I'm ready to go home.

Acknowledgements

I wish, first, to acknowledge the Martu people of Jigalong, the custodians of the land on which I lived and worked, and to thank them for all that they taught me.

I am grateful to Dr Jill Durey of Edith Cowan University for her belief that this memoir had value, and for her gentle advice, encouragement and guidance in seeing it to completion. Thanks to Dr Gary Partington, for his valuable insights into the lives of Aboriginal people.

I acknowledge the work of Professor Robert Tonkinson, which provided the basis of my understanding of the culture and history of the Martu people.

I owe a debt of gratitude to Sandy Cornall for her friendship while we were at Jigalong and afterwards, and to the late Jim Marsh for his generous mentoring and assistance.

Tom Wilson helped me to find my voice.

A number of people helped me during the preparation of *Other People's Country* and I am grateful for their kindness. I would like to thank my children and grandchildren. Special thanks are due to my daughter, Annie O'Callaghan and friends Elizabeth Brennan, Helen Smith Burston and Jono Burston, Christina Houen, Diana Johnson, Rosemary Keenan, Helen McMahon, Coral Newman, and Beverley Winton. They not only encouraged me over the years, but also read various drafts and offered generous encouragement, thoughtful comments and suggestions.

I'm grateful to Ali Lavau for her enthusiastic response to my manuscript and for her sensitive and careful editing. Finally, my thanks to Jo Mackay of ABC Books for her wisdom and good humoured guidance in the process of publishing this book.